HISTC
OF
KILLEEN CASTLE
COUNTY MEATH,
IRELAND

MARY-ROSE CARTY

ASSISTED BY: D. W. LYNCH
M. J. LYNCH
M. J. A. MULVANY

KILLEEN: Cillín, a small church

Published by: Carty/Lynch, Dunsany, Co. Meath, Ireland
April 1991, reprinted April 2000
Revised Edition 2008

Cover illustration: Michael O'Brien, Kilmessan, Co. Meath

Cover design: Stuart Gray, Dunshaughlin, Co. Meath

Typesetting: A & J Print Dunshaughlin Ltd.

ISBN 978-0-9517382-0-7
EAN 9780951738207

Printed in Ireland by
Colour Books Ltd., Baldoyle, Dublin 13

The undertaking of this mammoth task of writing the History of the Earls of Fingall, has been achieved by Mary Rose Carty.

Her years of careful and diligent research, with the help of documents, letters, libraries and friends, have been worthwhile, producing a book which is both historically factual and rewarding. I congratulate Mary Rose and her helpers and wish them every success in this interesting addition to Irish History.

Clair, Countess of Fingall

Clair Fingall

January, 1991

CONTENTS

Historical  Context

Killeen Castle, North View

1981 Paul Tierney

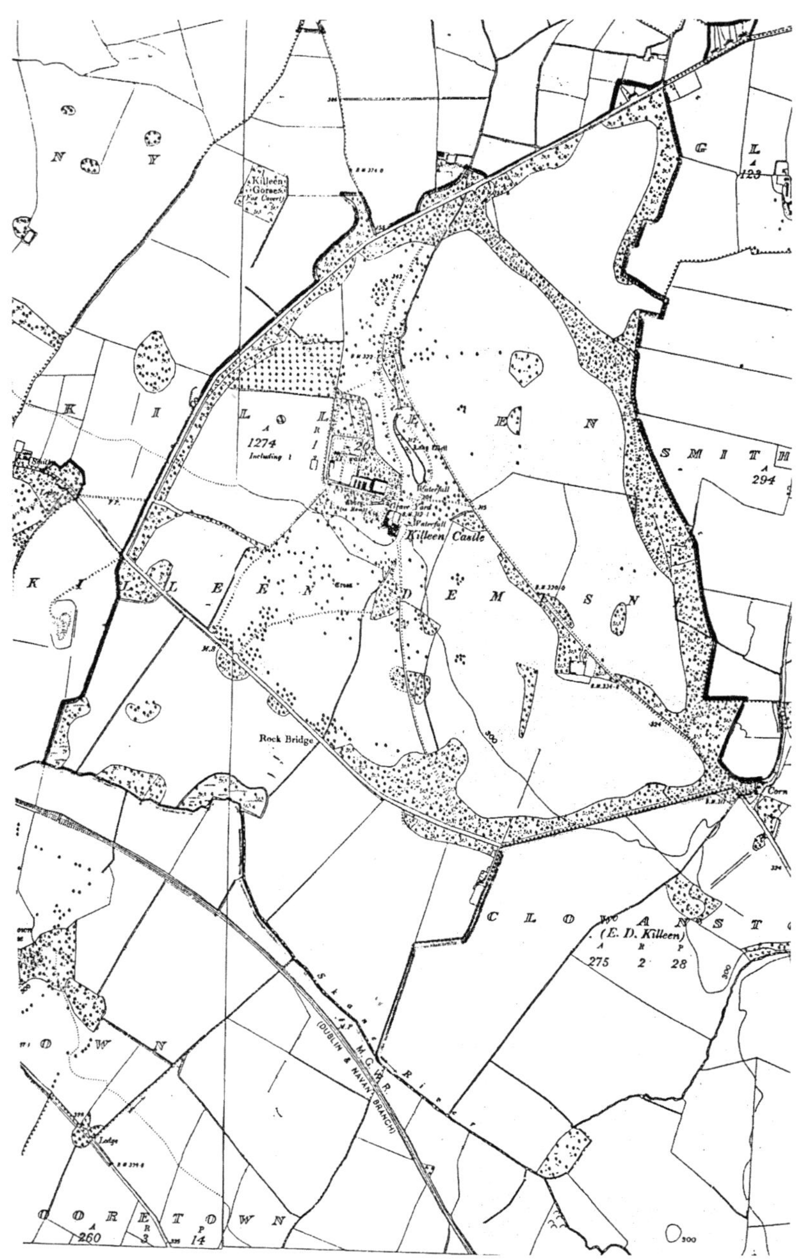

Surveyed in1836. Revised in 1909.
Based on the Ordnance Survey by
permission of the Government (Permit No. 5385)

By Paul Tierney

Our history of Killeen begins in 1169 with the Norman Invasion of Ireland. Diarmuid McMurrough, King of Leinster, a small kingdom in the South East of Ireland, sought Henry II's help in recovering his kingdom, which had been taken from him by Rory O'Connor, High King of Ireland.

Henry was too busy securing his own lands in France, but, seeing an opportunity to extend his possessions, gave permission to Diarmuid to seek the aid of his nobles in Wales. In 1169, and again in 1170, Norman armies arrived in Ireland and gained possession of Waterford, Wexford and Dublin.

Anxious lest these nobles should become too powerful, Henry came to Ireland in 1172. He accepted the homage of his nobles and many of the Irish Chieftains. To them he made grants of land, thus introducing feudalism to Ireland.

Meath was given to Hugh de Lacy, and he in turn divided his fief among his nobles. Each of these knights was given the title Baron and the land they were granted was called a Barony.

The Barony of Skryne was given to Adam de Feipo, and Adam gave Killeen to Geoffrey de Cusack.

CHARTER OF HENRY II

'Henry, by the grace of God, King of England, Duke of Normandy and Aquitaine, and Earl of Anjou, to the Archbishops, Bishops, Abbots, Earls, Barons, Justices and to all his Ministers and faithful subjects, French, English and Irish, of all his dominions, greetings: Know ye, that I have given and granted, and by this my charter confirmed unto Hugh de Lacy, in consideration of his services, the land of Meath, with the appurtenances; to have and to hold for me and my heirs, to him and his heirs, by the service of fifty knights, in as full and ample manner as Murchard Hy-Melaghlin held it, or any other person before him or after him. And as an addition I give him all fees, which he owes or shall owe to me about Dublin, while he is my bailiff, to do me service in my City of Dublin. Wherefore I will and strictly command, that the said Hugh and his heirs shall enjoy the same land, and shall hold all the liberties and free customs which I have or may have therein, by the aforesaid service, from me and my heirs well and peaceably, freely, quietly and honourably, in wood and plain, in meadows and pastures, in waters and mills, in warrens and ponds, in fishings and huntings, in ways and paths, in seaports and all other places and things appertaining to the said land, with all liberties which I have therein or can grant or confirm to him by this my charter.

Witness Earl Richard, son of Gilbert,
William de Braosa, etc., at Wexford.'
1172

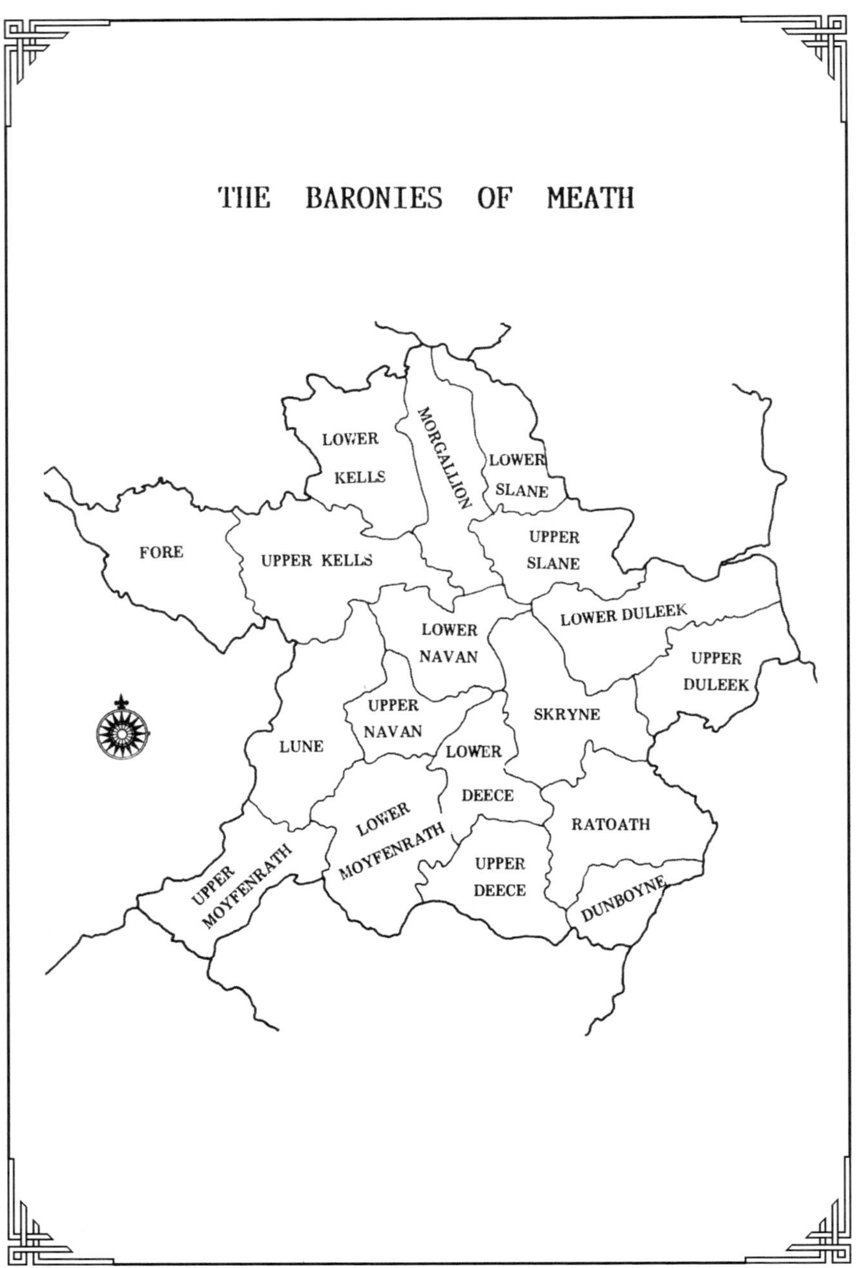

By Paul Tierney

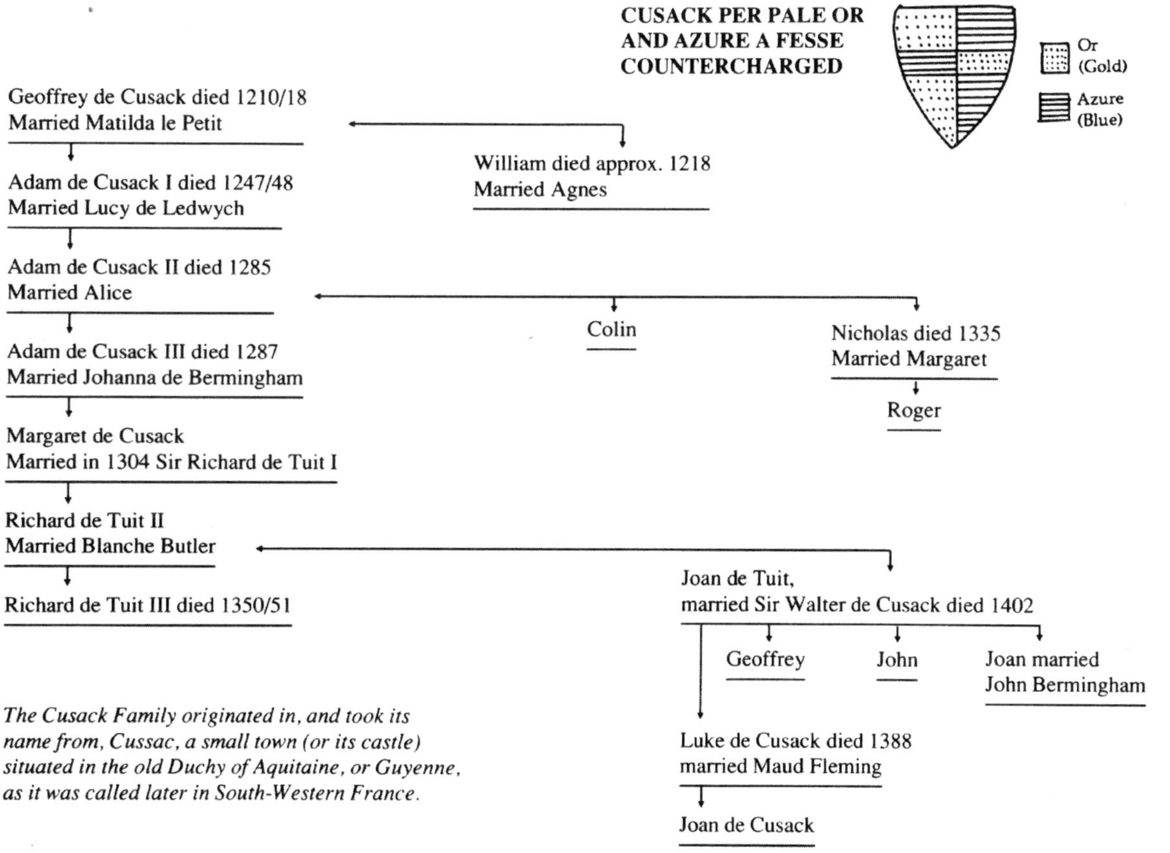

The Cusack Family originated in, and took its name from, Cussac, a small town (or its castle) situated in the old Duchy of Aquitaine, or Guyenne, as it was called later in South-Western France.

1ST 'LORD OF KILLEEN'	Geoffrey de Cusack married Matilda daughter of Adam le Petit
2ND 'LORD OF KILLEEN'	Adam de Cusack I married Lucy, daughter of Roger de Ledwych
3RD 'LORD OF KILLEEN'	Adam de Cusack II married Alicia
4TH 'LORD OF KILLEEN'	Adam de Cusack III married Johanna de Bermingham, daughter of the Baron of Athenry
5TH 'LORD OF KILLEEN'	Richard de Tuit I married Margaret, daughter and heir of Adam de Cusack III
6TH 'LORD OF KILLEEN'	Richard de Tuit II married Blanche, daughter of the Earl of Ormond
7TH 'LORD OF KILLEEN'	Richard de Tuit III
8TH 'LORD OF KILLEEN'	Sir Walter de Cusack married Joan, sister and heir of Richard de Tuit III
9TH 'LORD OF KILLEEN'	Sir Luke de Cusack married Maud, daughter of Sir Simon Fleming

GEOFFREY DE CUSACK would appear to have come over from France to assist Hugh de Lacy to colonise Meath about 1175. His immediate overlord was Adam de Feipo and Geoffrey became lord of the Manor of Killeen, Co. Meath. (It is possible that Adam de Feipo and Geoffrey were related.)

Over the door of Killeen Castle the date of its building is given as 1181.

Geoffrey married Matilda, daughter/sister of Adam le Petit, and they are known to have had two sons: Adam, who carried on the main line, and William. Geoffrey made several grants to religious houses.

His death is estimated between 1210 and 1218.

(It is possible that Geoffrey had three sons - Geoffrey Óg, Adam and William. This would mean that Geoffrey II inherited Killeen first and that Adam inherited after the death of his brother.)

TRIM CASTLE (KING JOHN'S CASTLE) WAS BUILT
JERUSALEM WAS CAPTURED BY THE TURKS IN 1187
THE THIRD CRUSADE TOOK PLACE
THE MAGNA CARTA WAS AGREED
ROBIN HOOD WAS OUTLAWED IN SHERWOOD FOREST

ADAM DE CUSACK I married Lucy, daughter of Roger de Ledwych, who brought him as dowry the land of Slevene, given by her brother. By a charter of 1230, Adam de Ledwych, brother of Lucy, granted all the land held by his father and by himself in the honour of Duleek, in the valley of the Any, to Sir Adam de Cusack and Lucy, his wife, in exchange for the land of Slevene originally granted by him.

In 1238 Sir Adam was granted permission to hold a market at Killeen. He also attested many grants to religious houses.

Sir Adam and Lucy had a son, Adam II, and, possibly, other children. He was a knight and would have spent much of his life as a soldier.

Adam I was involved in a dispute in Mayo, where he claimed a Manor in the townland of Carn to the west of Killala Bay. He died 1247/1248, possibly killed in Mayo.

THE ANGLO-NORMANS WERE EXTENDING THEIR RULE INTO CONNAUGHT
THE ENGLISH PARLIAMENT BEGAN TO PLAY AN IMPORTANT PART IN THE (RULE) GOVERNMENT

ADAM DE CUSACK II married Alice (Alicia). He is known to have had three sons: Adam III, Nicholas and Colin.

Adam is said to have served on juries and possibly held public office. He died 1285.

THE BATTLE OF CALLANN 1261
WALES WAS FINALLY CONQUERED BY THE ANGLO-NORMANS
ST. THOMAS AQUINAS, 1225-1275
LOUIS IX (ST. LOUIS), 1226-1270

ADAM DE CUSACK III is mentioned in the Justiciary Rolls regarding a dispute over land in the barony of Tirawley, in North Connaught, and held the Manor of Cullina (in the later parish of Kilmormoy, Co.Mayo).

Adam married Johanna de Bermingham, daughter of the Baron of Athenry. Johanna brought as her dowry Bonefinn and Drynaghbeg, in the barony of Tireragh, Co. Sligo.

He seems to have been a professional soldier during his long minority. Adam's reign as lord of Killeen was short. He died in 1287 leaving Margaret, his only child, as heir. Johanna lived to at least 1305.

RICHARD DE TUIT I married Margaret de Cusack, heir of Adam III, on the 4th November, 1304, and became lord of Killeen by right of his wife. (Margaret, the only child and heir, was a minor when her father died and became the ward of Simon de Feipo, the overlord, before 1290.) Sir Richard was of Logloth (modern Ballyloughloe), Co. Westmeath. Margaret died 1312.

THE 'MODEL PARLIAMENT' MET TO GRANT MONEY FOR WAR AGAINST THE SCOTS AND FRENCH
BABYLONIAN CAPTIVITY OF PAPACY, 1309-1376

RICHARD DE TUIT II inherited Killeen and his mother's other lands. He married Blanche Bulter, daughter of the Earl of Ormond, and had two children, Richard and Joan.

RICHARD DE TUIT III succeeded to Killeen but died 1350/1351 without leaving an heir. His sister, Joan, succeeded.

BRUCE INVASION OF IRELAND
BLACK DEATH THROUGHOUT EUROPE 1348-1349
DANTE WROTE *THE DIVINE COMEDY*

SIR WALTER DE CUSACK married Joan de Tuit, in the 1340s, and became lord of Killeen and Clonee, by right of his wife. Sir Walter was from Gerardstown, parish of Kilcarne, barony of Skryne.

Joan had her marriage dissolved prior to 1364 by the Bishop of Meath (on the grounds that, before marriage to her, Walter cohabited with a woman related to her in the third degree of kindred). She married Sir Henry Ferrers, who had a manor in Clonee; however, on a visit of the Archbishop of Armagh, Walter suggested that his marriage had been valid and, subsequently, the prelate declared the marriage valid and Joan was ordered to go back and live with Walter as his wife.

Joan and Henry appealed to Pope Urban V in 1364 and he called for a report. Whatever the outcome, Joan did not return and a violent struggle over her inheritance took place. Walter evicted Henry and Joan from her estate by armed force. He was evidently afraid that if they had children they might manage to succeed. On her death, however, Luke de Cusack, her son by Sir Walter de Cusack, inherited Killeen.

Sir Walter married, secondly, Elizabeth (surname unknown). He died prior to 1402.

1366 STATUTES OF KILKENNY
RICHARD II VISITS IRELAND
100 YEARS' WAR WAS RAGING BETWEEN ENGLAND AND FRANCE
CHAUCER (1340-1400) WROTE *CANTERBURY TALES*

SIR LUKE DE CUSACK inherited Killeen on his mother's death. On the 1st March, 1372, he was granted letters patent giving him the right to hold a market every week, on a Monday, in his Manor of Killeen, by King Edward III.

He was knighted before 1382 and died shortly after September, 1388, having married Matilda (Maud), daughter of Sir Simon Fleming. He left an only child, Joan, who married Sir Christopher Plunkett. From then on the name Plunkett became synonymous with Killeen.

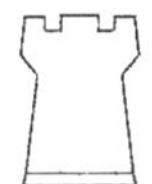

Sable (Black)

Argent (Silver)

PLUNKETT
Sable a bend argent,
in the sinister point.
A tower, triple towered,
of the last.
Supporters, a pegasus
and an antelope

JOAN DE CUSACK
MARRIED SIR CHRISTOPHER PLUNKETT IN 1403

- John died in his father's lifetime married Elizabeth Holywode
  - Christopher, died 1462. Married Joanna Bellew
    - Christopher married Elizabeth Wells
      - daughter married Nicholas, 16th Baron of Howth
    - Edmund, died 1510 married Elinor Fleming
      - John married 1st Margaret Preston, 2nd Ellen Barnewall
        - Patrick, died 1556 No Heir
        - Christopher married Alice Barnewall
          - Maud married Baron of Louth
          - Catherine married David Sutton
          - Margaret married Nicholas Aylmer
        - Henry
        - James, died 1595 married Margaret FitzGerald
          - Christopher, died 1616 married Genet Dillon
            - Lucas
            - Patrick, Bishop of Meath
            - Nicholas married Jane Dillon
            - James
        - Patrick
        - Margaret
    - Broughton
- Christopher founded House of Dunsany
- Thomas founded House of Rathmore
- Robert (Rowland) founded House of Dunsoghly
- Richard
- Edward founded House of Balrath
- Edmund became a priest

An account of the Plunkett family's arrival in Meath taken from *View of the Legal Institutions, Honorary Hereditary Offices and Feudal Baronies Established in the Reign of Henry II;* William Lynch, Pub. 1830.

"Richard Plunket, brother of John, Lord of Beaulieu, besides a considerable paternal estate, made large acquirements by his connexion with the families of Blundus, or Le Blunt, Lord of Rathregan, (who was summoned by writ to the Parliament of 1310), Le Tuite and Cusack. His son and heir, Richard, called Richard Plunket Junior, was Lord of Rathregan, Tullaghanogue, and Killallon; and on the 14th of March 1358, by a deed in the French language, Lionel the King's son, by the title of 'Lionell Fitz, a noble Roi Dengleterre & de Fraunce, Comit D'Ulnestre & Seigneur de Connaught,' appointed his dear and well beloved Roger de Heygham and Richard Plunket his Attornies General, to do and answer in all things for him in Ireland, and to hold his courts by themselves or their deputies in his Barony of Ratowth and seignoiry of Coly, etc. This appointment, which was, according to the practice of that day, a sort of deputation of power to represent the prince who gave it, rendered Richard Plunket one of the most influential lords within the Pale, by placing under his authority the provinces of Ulster and Connaught, which were then separate jurisdictions, exclusively belonging to Lionel, Duke of Clarence. There are various entries to be found by which it appears that Lord Richard's possessions were extremely extensive; and by the settlement of the Loughgower, Moreton, Dunshaughlin, and other estates belonging to the family of Berford, his sons were made remainder men in tail male to those estates.

When a Parliament was summoned in the year 1374, a writ was issued to him, as well as to Walter Cusack, Baron of Killeen, amongst the other Earls, Magnates, and Proceres of Ireland; and on that occasion, it should be observed, his kinsman Richard Plunket, already mentioned, was summoned amongst the Lord's assistant or Members of the King's Privy Council. He died soon after this Parliament; and it appears by certain entails that he had two sons, John and Christopher; the former of whom must have died without issue, as his name occurs not after that period.

Christopher was a minor at his father's death; and it was not until 1391 that he was sued to take on him the order of knighthood, according to law; for which purpose he was found by inquisition to possess the necessary qualifications in the county of Meath alone. At this time the title of the family, we should conclude, was Baron of Rathregan, as it was there Lord Richard and his son resided; and the castle of Rathregan, as the place of residence, must be considered to have been the 'caput barony'; but soon after, Sir Christopher Plunket married Johanna the daughter and heiress of Sir Lucas Cusack, Baron of Killeen, the son and heir of Sir Walter Cusack, Chevalier, who was summoned by writ to several parliaments, and particularly to that of the 48th of Edward the Third, to which Richard Plunket was summoned at the same time. By this marriage Sir Christopher acquired, in right of his wife, Lady Johanna, the lordships and manors of Killeen, Kilskeer, Killallon, Clonmacduffe and Clony, with advowsons of the churches lying within the same. This marriage took place in or before the year 1402, while parliamentary dignities, as declared in the 51st. Edw. III., were enjoyed by tenure, as on the 3rd May in the former year, Sir Christopher and his wife were ordered to be released from the debt of £300, for which her father and grandfather, Sir Walter and Sir Lucas, stood bound to the King by bond, in consideration chiefly of Sir Christopher's labours, and expenses incurred, when accompanying the Lord Lieutenant in various journeys. But to obtain legal possession of the seigniories accruing to him by this marriage, Sir Christopher and Lady Johanna were obliged to sue out several charters or letters patent, whereby the King forgave and remitted the penalties imposable on those who married the King's wards, or entered on their possessions, without royal licence; and accordingly Henry the Fourth, Henry the Fifth, and Henry the Sixth, granted several such pardons, now enrolled, to the said Sir Christopher and Johanna his wife, remitting all actions, penalties, and fines for this marriage, and for entering into the manors of Killeen, Kilskeer, Killallon, &c. In these records, which were tantamount to a new gift from the Crown of the seigniories, and in several others entered on the Exchequer rolls, the marriage, the estates, and the descent of Johanna from Sir Walter the grandfather, are set forth. Soon after this, Sir Christopher changed his residence to Killeen castle, where he thenceforward resided."

1ST BARON KILLEEN	Sir Christopher Plunkett married Joan, daughter and heir of Sir Luke de Cusack
	John Plunkett married Elizabeth, daughter of Holywode of Artane, Co. Dublin. (He died during his father's lifetime)
2ND BARON KILLEEN	Sir Christopher Plunkett married Joanna, daughter of Bellew of Bellewstown, Co. Meath
3RD BARON KILLEEN	Sir Christopher Plunkett married Elizabeth, daughter of Sir William Wells
4TH BARON KILLEEN	Sir Edmund Plunkett, brother of Sir Christopher Plunkett, married Elinor Fleming, daughter of Lord Fleming
5TH BARON KILLEEN	Sir John Plunkett married 1st Margaret Preston; married 2nd Ellen Barnewall
6TH BARON KILLEEN	Sir Patrick Plunkett
7TH BARON KILLEEN	Sir Christopher Plunkett, brother of Patrick Plunkett, married Alice, daughter of Sir Christopher Barnewall
8TH BARON KILLEEN	Sir James Plunkett, brother of Patrick and Christopher Plunkett, married Margery, daughter of Richard FitzGerald
9TH BARON KILLEEN	Sir Christopher Plunkett married Genet, daughter of Sir Lucas Dillon

SIR CHRISTOPHER PLUNKETT of Rathregan (near Batterstown, Co. Meath) married Joan, daughter and heir of Sir Luke de Cusack in 1401/02, and, in her right, became lord of Killeen.

The Plunkett Family was of Danish origin and possibly arrived in Ireland as early as the tenth century. Sir Christopher's ancestors had settled in Bewley, Co. Louth. His grandfather Richard Plunkett, had established the House of Rathregan. It is said 'when the Normans invaded Ireland the Plunketts did not join them as they knew they were going to win, but, subsequently, married them and became their Bishops and Lawyers and, later, their Barons'.

Sir Christopher Plunkett and Lady Joan had seven sons and three daughters. The eldest, John, was heir of Killeen; the second Christopher, founded the House of Dunsany, Co. Meath; Thomas, the third son, founded the House of Rathmore, Co. Meath (between Navan and Athboy); Robert founded the House of Dunsoghly, Co. Dublin (St. Margaret's); Richard died without family; Edward founded the House of Balrath, Co. Meath (between Clonmellon and Kells); and Edmund became a priest.

Early in the fifteenth century, Sir Christopher and his wife erected the present old church of Killeen, most probably on the site of its predecessor. In the west end of the Chancel they founded a Chantry consisting of four priests to have the Holy Sacrifice of the Mass offered up for the souls of their ancestors and the spiritual welfare of their family.

In 1426 Christopher received a sum of money from Henry VI, as recompense for the services he had rendered in the wars of Ireland. Before this time he was Sheriff of Meath and, in 1432, was deputy to Sir Thomas Stanley, Knt., Lord Lieutenant of Ireland.

Sir Christopher Plunkett was a peer, not just a feudal Lord of the Manor, and was created Baron, by writ, between 1403 and 1445. (It has not been possible to find an exact date for the writ but it would probably have been 1436.)

The first Baron of Killeen died in 1445.

100 YEARS' WAR CONTINUED
JOAN OF ARC LEAD THE FRENCH RESURGENCE, AND WAS FINALLY CAPTURED AND BURNED AT THE STAKE, 1431

SIR JOHN PLUNKETT did not succeed, having died during his father's lifetime. He married Elizabeth Holywode, daughter of Holywode of Artane, Co. Dublin. He left a son and heir.

SIR CHRISTOPHER PLUNKETT succeeded his grandfather, and married Joanna, daughter of Bellew of Bellewstown, by whom he had three sons. The youngest, Broughton, fell at the Battle of Stoke in 1487, fighting for Lambert Simnel.

Sir Christopher died in 1462.

PRINTING PRESS WAS DEVELOPED IN GUTENBURG
CONSTANTINOPLE CAPTURED BY THE TURKS
WARS OF THE ROSES IN ENGLAND

SIR CHRISTOPHER PLUNKETT, Baron Killeen, was summoned to Parliament in 1463. He married Elizabeth, daughter of Sir William Wells, Lord Chancellor of Ireland. Sir Christopher died before 1470, and leaving no heir, only a daughter who could not inherit, as the writ conferring the Barony had stipulated 'male heirs of the body', was succeeded by his brother, Edmund.

POYNING'S PARLIAMENT IN IRELAND
CIVIL WAR IN ENGLAND

SIR EDMUND PLUNKETT became Baron of Killeen. He married Elinor Fleming, daughter of Lord Fleming, and died 18th August, 1510, leaving a son and heir.

DISCOVERY OF THE NEW WORLD 1492
HENRY VII, KING OF ENGLAND
KILDARE GERALDINES LEADING
ANGLO-NORMAN FAMILY
LEONARDO DA VINCI

SIR JOHN PLUNKETT was sworn to the Privy Council of Henry VIII. He married first Margaret Preston, by whom he had a son, Patrick. Secondly, Ellen Barnewall, by whom he had Christopher, Henry, James and a daughter, Margaret. Sir John Plunkett died 19th March, 1550.

REIGNS OF HENRY VIII & EDWARD VI
DISSOLUTION OF IRISH MONASTERIES
REFORMATION IN EUROPE

SIR PATRICK PLUNKETT died without an heir, about 1556, and was succeeded by his brother.

PLANTATION OF LEIX AND OFFALY
COUNCIL OF TRENT
MARY I, QUEEN OF ENGLAND

SIR CHRISTOPHER PLUNKETT, sat in the Parliament of 1559. He married Alice, daughter of Sir Christopher Barnewall, Knt., of Crickstown, Co. Meath, and left three daughters. Maud married the Baron of Louth; Catherine married David Sutton of Castletown, who was attainted and beheaded for rebellion in 1574 with Viscount Baltinglas; and Margaret married Nicholas Aylmer. Christopher was succeeded by his brother.

KNOX IN SCOTLAND
MICHELANGELO
HUGUENOT PERSECUTION IN FRANCE

SIR JAMES PLUNKETT, whose inheritance was not opposed by the daughters of his deceased brother, Christopher, succeeded. He took his place in the House of Peers in the year 1585. He married Margery, daughter of Richard FitzGerald of Fyanstown, Co. Meath, and died 13th January, 1595, having had five sons and three daughters. His eldest son, Christopher, succeeded.

QUEEN ELIZABETH I OF ENGLAND
SHAKESPEARE
SPANISH ARMADA
9 YEARS' WAR IN IRELAND

SIR CHRISTOPHER PLUNKETT sat in Parliament. He married Genet, daughter of Sir Lucas Dillon, and left, at his decease on the 12th October, 1613, an eldest son, Lucas, who became 1st Earl of Fingall, Patrick, who became Bishop of Meath, Nicholas, who became an eminent barrister, and James.

ENGLISH EAST INDIA COMPANY CHARTERED
IRISH DEFEAT AT KINSALE
JAMES I ASCENDS THRONE 1603
ULSTER PLANTATION

Festina Lente
(Hasten Slowly)

LUCAS PLUNKETT, DIED 1637
married 1st Elizabeth O'Donnell
2nd Susannah Brabazon
3rd Eleanor Bagenal
4th Margaret Nicholas St. Lawrence

ARMS – Sa., a bend, arg.; in the sinister chief a tower, triple-towered, of the second. Crest – a horse, passant, arg. Supporters – dextor, a pegasus, per fesse, or and arg.; sinister, an antelope, arg., horned, unguled, gorged with a plain collar, and chained, or.
Motto: Festina Lente (interpreted as 'Hasten with Caution')

Book Plate

Christopher, died 1641
married Mabel Barnewall

George married Cicely Hill

James married
1st Catherine Plunkett (niece of St. Oliver Plunkett)
2nd Mary Cusack

Luke, died 1649
married Margaret Donough

Peter, died 1717
married Frances Hales

Elizabeth married
Rowland Eyre

Helena married
1st Sir FitzGerald Alymer
2nd Michael Fleming

Amelia married Theobald
Earl of Carlingford

Justin, died 1734
married Mary Fitzgerald

no heir

Margaret married
J. Nugent

Emelia married
Robert, Earl Nugent

Mary married
1st Maurice O'Connor
2nd Robert FitzGerald

Robert, died 1738
married Mary Magenis

Mary married
William O'Mara

Arthur James, died 1793
married Henrietta Wollascot

Luke

Anne married
William Saltmarsh

Arthur James, died 1836
married Frances Donelan

Luke

Robert

William

Theresa married
James Dease

Arthur James, died 1869
married Louisa Emilia Corbally

Harriet married
John Jones

Arthur James, died 1881
married Elise Mary Rio

Elias Robert

William Matthew

Edmund Luke

George John

Francis Richard
married May Tevis
dau. of C. W. Morgan
Philadelphia

Emma Francis
married William
Maurice Anderton

Henrietta married
Thomas W. C. Riddall

Arthur James Francis, died 1929
married Elizabeth Mary Margaret Burke

Mary Louisa married
George FitzGerald Murphy

Henrietta Marie married
Robert Bernard
Ashhurst Gradwell

Oliver James Horace, died 1984
married 1st Jessica Hughes
2nd Clair H. Richardson

Mary Elizabeth married
Cyril Gage Pardo Kirk

Henrietta
Maria

Gerald William Desmond

Elizabeth
married Peter Wood

John Oliver Pardo Kirk
married Penelope Anne Gradidge

Jessica Anne

Charles Reggie

1ST EARL OF FINGALL	Lucas Plunkett married 1st Elizabeth, daughter of Rory O'Donnell (Earl of Tyrconnell); married 2ndly Susannah, daughter of Edward, Lord Brabazon; married 3rdly Eleanor, daughter of Dudley Bagenal; married 4thly Margaret, daughter of Nicholas St. Lawrence
2ND EARL OF FINGALL	Christopher Plunkett married Mabel, daughter of Nicholas, Viscount Barnewall
3RD EARL OF FINGALL	Luke Plunkett married Margaret, daughter of Donough, Earl of Clancarty
4TH EARL OF FINGALL	Peter Plunkett married Frances, daughter of Sir Edward Hales
5TH EARL OF FINGALL	Justin Plunkett married Mary, daughter of Maurice Fitzgerald
6TH EARL OF FINGALL	Robert Plunkett married Mary, daughter of Roger Magenis
7TH EARL OF FINGALL	Arthur James Plunkett married Henrietta Marie, daughter of William Wollascott
8TH EARL OF FINGALL	Arthur James Plunkett married Frances, daughter of John Donelan
9TH EARL OF FINGALL	Arthur James Plunkett married Louisa Emilia, daughter of Elias Corbally
10TH EARL OF FINGALL	Arthur James Plunkett married Elise Mary, daughter of Francis Alexis Rio
11TH EARL OF FINGALL	Arthur James Francis Plunkett married Elizabeth Mary, daughter of George Burke
12TH EARL OF FINGALL	Oliver James Horace Plunkett married 1st Jessica, daughter of Alan Hughes; married 2nd Clair Hilda, daughter of Dr. Henry Salmon

Fingall comes from 'Fionn Gaill' - meaning 'Fair Foreigners' (many of the Norse invaders settled in the district north of Dublin, and in time, the district itself came to be called Fingal).

LUCAS, 1st Earl of Fingall: This nobleman had a large grant of territory in 1618, and was created Earl of Fingall on the 26th September, 1628, by Charles I. Preluding the honour, the King wrote a most flattering letter, dated Westminster, 28th June that year, beginning 'That having received good testimonies of the virtuous and many good parts of his right trusty and well beloved subject, the Lord Baron Killeen, being one of the ancient nobility of Ireland, His Majesty was pleased...'.

In a Deed of Purchase, dated 21st November, 1622, the Co. Cavan estate passed to Sir Hugh Clume.

The Earl married first Elizabeth, daughter of Rory O'Donnell, Earl of Tyrconnell, by whom he had no heir. He married secondly Susannah, daughter of Edward, Lord Brabazon, and had Christopher, his heir, and George. His Lordship married thirdly Eleanor (widow of Sir Thomas Colclough), daughter of Dudley Bagnel of Dunleckny, Co. Carlow. Eleanor died November, 1632. Fourthly, the Earl married Margaret, daughter of Nicholas St. Lawrence, Lord Howth. She was also a widow, having been married first to Jenico Preston, Viscount Gormanston. Margaret died November, 1637

Lucas, Earl of Fingall, died 29th March, 1637.

CHARLES I
30 YEARS' WAR 1618-1648
MAYFLOWER SAILS FROM PLYMOUTH

CHRISTOPHER, 2nd Earl of Fingall, married in January, 1636, Hon. Mabel Barnewall, daughter of Nicholas, 1st Viscount Barnewall of Kingsland. He had a son and heir, Luke.

The Earl, who, with other Catholic Lords, was outlawed in the County of Meath on the 17th November, 1641, took a prominent part, as Commander of Horse, in the war which broke out in that year. He was a leading figure in the gatherings at Tara and Duleek, and was involved in the siege of Drogheda in 1642; altogether he was outlawed seven times. Ultimately, he was taken prisoner after the Battle of Rathmines in which the Cromwellian, Jones, defeated the Earl of Ormonde on 2nd August, 1649. Fourteen days later he died in Dublin Castle, and was buried in St. Catherine's, Dublin, on the 18th August, 1649.

His widow, Mabel, married Colonel James Barnewall in 1653, and died at Beggstown. She was buried in Killeen on the 4th February, 1699.

CONFEDERATION OF KILKENNY
BATTLES AT BENBURB & DUNGAN'S HILL
EXECUTION OF CHARLES I
CROMWELL 1653-1658

LUKE, 3rd Earl of Fingall, was born in 1639, and following his father's death (Killeen and the family estates having been forfeited) lived for a time with Dr. Patrick Plunkett, later Bishop of Meath, and Sir Nicholas Plunkett (great-uncles of the Earl's) as an exile in France and Flanders.

In 1663 a Decree of Innocency was issued by the Court of Claims for Luke, Earl of Fingall. The court ordered the restoration of all lands and tenements claimed by him, except the following:

'Nodstowne, Reynoldstowne, Drumbarragh, Destinrath, Catleoghtowne, Maperath, Curragh and Cloneenane, Cornesose, Mote, Rathenrick, Loghham, Cabragh and part of Fagenstowne, Co. Meath, a house in Drogheda, a parcel of arable land in Ardee, a house in Oxmanstowne called "Fingall House" and a parcel of land called "Scurloggsland" adjoining Drumbarr, Co. Meath.'

On the 26th March, 1672, further land was reverted to Luke, Earl of Fingall, in Cos. Cavan and Meath 'to hold of Dublin Castle, in free and common socage, at rents payable only after the death, without heirs male of his body, of the Patentee.'

Luke married Margaret, daughter of Donough, Earl of Clancarty and had three daughters, Elizabeth, Helena and Amelia, and a son, Peter.

Letters patent were issued to Luke, Earl of Fingall, for a weekly market on Saturdays and two yearly fairs, 24th/25th June and 18th/19th October, at Killeen, by Charles II on 14th August, 1672.

Luke left a will dated 10th November, 1685, in which he bequeathed to his daughters £100 a year, 'until their portions were paid'; with an additional £2,000 each if his son, Peter, Lord Killeen, died without issue. To his wife, Margaret, he left the castle and lands of Killeen for her life, with whatever was required out of the estate to bring her jointure up to

£600. To his brothers, Edward and Nicholas, £100, to his Uncle George, an annuity of £10, to his servant, Christopher Archbold, £50 and to Dame Butler, £100. His wife was to manage the person and estate of his son during minority.

He appointed as executors: his wife, his mother, Mabel, Countess Dowager of Fingall, Jenico Preston and Viscount Gormanston.

Margaret, Countess of Fingall, died the 1st January, 1703.

'POPISH' PLOT AGAINST LONDON PARLIAMENT
EXECUTION OF ST. OLIVER PLUNKETT 1681
JAMES II ASCENDS THE THRONE

PETER, 4th Earl of Fingall, was born in 1678. This nobleman was outlawed by the name 'Luke' for his loyalty to his legitimate sovereign, James II, but the outlawry was reversed six years after in 1697.

He married Frances, daughter of Sir Edward Hales.

There is a marriage settlement, dated 7th September, 1698 in respect of Peter, Earl of Fingall, and Frances, one of the daughters of Sir Edward Hales, Bt., late of St. Stephens, Kent, and sister of Sir John Hales of Tenterden, Kent, Bt., 'Portion £4,000; jointure £600, to be raised out of all the lands which include the lordship of Killeene, the manor of Killallan, the manor of Rathregan and the lordship and manor of Killskerr.

Remainders (failing heirs male of the body of the Earl) to his uncle, Nicholas Plunkett, Esq., his great-uncle, George Plunkett, Esq., the heirs of "James, sometime Lord Baron of Killeene" and the heirs of "the lord Baron of Killeene" who was grandfather to the said James.'

Peter and Frances had three daughters, Margaret, Emilia and Mary, also an only son, Justin.

At the beginning of the eighteenth century the 4th Earl was one of the largest Catholic landowners in Ireland. He died 24th January, 1717.

('A Light to the Blind', handwritten, and in two volumes, was presented by the 12th Earl of Fingall, in 1934, to the National Library. Although the work is now credited to Nicholas Plunkett, *circa* 1720, according to family tradition it was written by Peter, 4th Earl of Fingall. It is the work of an Irish Nationalist and devoted adherent of James II. The King's career is described and it contains vivid accounts of The Battle of the Boyne and Aughrim, and the subsequent capitulation at Limerick.)

The 4th Earl is also said to have 'appeared' in Killeen Castle, at various times, up to the early 1900s.

BATTLE OF THE BOYNE
WILLIAMITE LAND CONFISCATIONS
PENAL LAWS ENACTED
UNION OF SCOTLAND WITH ENGLAND 1707
LOUIS XIV, KING OF FRANCE

JUSTIN, 5th Earl of Fingall succeeded to the title on the 24th January, 1717.

There is an undated letter from Frances, Countess of Fingall (widow of the 4th Earl). It reads:

'Dear Uncle,

> Thank you for your trouble in arranging a scheme in order for the clearing of my Lord's debts without selling - I have desired the Earl of Aran to let me make use of his name to screen me from the law and to secure "him" from being bred a Protestant and am persuaded I could not make a better choice, being the next Protestant relation which is agreeable to law and that I'm well satisfied he will not give us any trouble about his religion - desire you'll send me proposals for my jointure of the ablest tenants which I would set for one year at the best advantage till I shall be able to go over.'

Justin married Mary, daughter of Maurice Fitzgerald of Castle Ishen, Co. Cork, in 1731.

Justin died in 1734 and Robert, his cousin and male heir, inherited.

1724 DEAN SWIFT'S *DRAPIER'S LETTERS*
PENAL LAWS IN IRELAND
COLONIAL RIVALRY GROWS BETWEEN FRANCE AND GREAT BRITAIN

ROBERT, 6th Earl of Fingall (grandson of George, second son of Lucas, 1st Earl). Robert's mother was a niece of Saint Oliver Plunkett. He inherited without opposition from the three daughters and heirs lineal of Peter, 4th Earl.

At the time Robert inherited, he was a Captain in Berwick's regiment in the service of France. He married Mary, daughter of Roger Magenis of the House of Iveagh, Co. Down, and died in 1738, in Paris, where he was interred. He left two sons, Arthur James and Luke, and a daughter Anne. His eldest son, Justin, had died as an infant.

REIGN OF GEORGE II
PENAL LAWS AGAINST RELIGIOUS PRACTICE NOT WIDELY ENFORCED BUT THOSE AGAINST CIVIL RIGHTS AND OWNERSHIP OF PROPERTY WERE

ARTHUR JAMES, 7th Earl of Fingall, was born in July, 1731 and brought up abroad. (His father would, in the normal course, have been some way out of the succession and had served in the Army in France making only occasional visits to Ireland in the 1730s).

Arthur was only seven when his father died and was placed under the guardianship of Charles, Earl of Arran, his nearest Protestant relative and, in some way that cannot be traced, had a second guardian who was a Catholic, Henry Howard of Greystoke in Cumberland.

In 1740 Arthur lost his mother, Mary Magenis.

Henry Howard appears, in spite of occasional trouble with the tenants, to have taken a share in the running of the Irish estate. Luke Dowdall (superintendent of the estate and manager of the minor's affairs in general) was also involved with the management, and found it loaded with heavy debts. Some of the tenants, taking advantage of Mr. Howard's incapacity to act as Guardian by reason of his religion, refused to pay their rents and a considerable part of the estate had been sold. At least three parts were sold while Arthur was still a minor, his Law Agent having failed to give notice of the proceedings. Portions of the estate were also due to Earl Justin's sisters.

> *'On Thursday, 19th March, 1755, at St. George's Church, Hanover Square, London, the Right Hon. Earl of Fingall of the Kingdom of Ireland, married Miss Henrietta Wollascott, only daughter and heir of William Wollascott, Esq., of Woolhampton in Berkshire.'*

Arthur James and Henrietta Maria shared the same faith, the Wollascott family having remained Catholic too despite the penalties and taxes imposed on them. Henrietta's father died in 1757 and the estate became part of the Fingall property. The Earl and Countess lived at Woolhampton after their marriage and press cuttings show that their children were born there. They had five children: Arthur James, Luke, Robert, William and Theresa.

In 1762 it was reported that 'the claim of the Earl of Fingall, to be restored to the Title and Honours of that Earldom, by taking off the attainder was, after hearing Counsel two days at the Bar of the House of Peers of Ireland, admitted by their Lordships and this young Nobleman will accordingly take his seat in that august assembly'.

The Countess of Fingall's mother, Henrietta Maria (daughter of Sir Baldwin Conyer) died at Woolhampton in 1770. The 7th Earl does not appear to have come to Ireland before this and was not living at Killeen until the 1780s. Killeen had not been lived in by any of the family since 1720, and Harrison reported in 1763 that 'everything about it has been a ruin for a great number of years and what remains of the old castle is but very small and not even capable of being made a habitation for a family'.

In May, 1778, the Earl wrote to his Agent, Patrick Dease, 'You'll please to remember that I am to be put into the possession of the Castle of Killeen tho' I shall permit the tenants to continue in it for this year'. From June, 1780 to November, 1781 there is a record of payments made to Ian Quinn, mason, for repairs to the castle.

A town residence was built about 1775 at 5 Great Denmark Street, Dublin, known as Killeen House. It is most likely that the Earl and his family moved to Dublin first. The Countess made inventories of household items and linens to be shipped to Dublin and later Killeen Castle. Henrietta endowed Killeen with many treasures including

Queen Anne furniture, silver and an immense quantity of old and valuable books. The castle library contained about 2,000 volumes.

Despite his absence, the 7th Earl was liked and respected. The Penal Laws would not have had a great impact upon a family of such standing as this and possibly afforded some protection to the parish of Killeen, as the parish records survived this stormy period.

The Earl sold the Woolhampton Estate in 1787, retaining possession of just over six acres in Upper Woolhampton, on which there were two sets of buildings. His chaplain remained at Woolhampton, receiving a small endowment with which he might keep himself and minister to the Catholic congregation, presumably founding what was known as the Woolhampton Catholic mission.

With the return of the Fingall family to Killeen Castle, a school was established by the Earl at Killeen with fee-paying and non fee-paying students.

ACCOUNTS BELONGING TO THE 7th EARL

1774	8 tons of coal £7.9s.4d. Subscription to three Rotunda Balls £2.16s.10½d. Two loads of hay 17s.4d.
1776	Henry Holden, weaver, of Naas for three sets of Damask table settings with Arms & Crests £20.0s.0d. Mr. Dalton, Coachmaker, for new paintings, new leathers, and other 'articles to the coach' £36.7s.1d.
1777	Abraham Bozier, half-year's wages £8.13s.4d. An excursion for 4 days into Co. Wicklow with 5 servants £9.0s.5d.
1780	Chance in the Lottery £2.5s.6d.
1783	Chair Hire in Dublin £1.1s.8d. Sword and Steel Belt 16s.0d.
1784	Taxes, exclusive of the demesne and my own farm, £236.12s.1d. A chestnut horse £19.0s.0d.
1790	Mr. Dempsey, Bread for three months in Dublin £12.17s.10½d.

Weekly labourers' bills 1789 to 1791 vary between £2.11s.8d in January and £10.9s.7d in September. The average number of men employed during these years was 30, and wages were from 4s.0d to 10s.0d per week (the carpenter being the highest paid).

Weekly bills, paid by Mr. John Flynn, totalled for the years:-

1781	£132. 9s. 4d.
1782	£431. 7s. 4d.
1783	£342. 14s. 7¼d.
1789	£626. 0s. 6½d.
1790	£496. 14s. 2½d.

His Lordship died 21st August, 1793 and Lady Henrietta 12th April, 1808.

CATHERINE THE GREAT OF RUSSIA
ANGER OVER STAMP ACT IN AMERICA
BOSTON TEA PARTY
AMERICAN DECLARATION OF INDEPENDENCE
FRENCH REVOLUTION
VOLUNTEERS IN IRELAND
COOK'S FIRST VOYAGE TO AUSTRALIA 1769

7th EARL, ARTHUR JAMES, a lease for a year to Randal, Lord Baron Dunsany & Sir Patrick Bellew, Bart.:

THIS INDENTURE made the fourteenth day of December in the year of our Lord one thousand seven hundred and eighty five Between Arthur James Plunkett the elder commonly called and who claims to be the Earl of Fingall in the Kingdom of Ireland on the one part and Randal Lord Baron Dunsany and Sir Patrick Bellew of Bermeath in the County of Louth Baronet of the other part Witnesseth that the said Arthur James Plunkett the Elder called Earl of Fingall for and in Consideration of the Sum of **Five Shillings sterling** to him in hand paid by the said Randal Lord Baron Dunsany and Sir Robert Bellew on the perfection hereof the receipt whereof they do and each of them doth hereby acknowledge he the said Arthur James Plunkett the Elder called Earl of Fingall Hath given granted bargained and sold and by these presents Doth give, grant, bargain and sell unto the said Randal Lord Baron of Dunsany and Sir Robert Bellew All that and those the Manor or Lordship or reputed Manor or Lordship of Killeen with the Rights, Royalties, Franchises, Liberties and Appurtenances thereunto belonging or in any wise Appertaining or therewith used occupied possessed or enjoyed And also All that and those the Towns and Lands of Geighanstown, Galboystown, Seraghstown, Milltown, Kilskeer Robinstown Surges otherewise Colledge Land. Foleystown Woodland, Kiltaile, Bellaghbane, Walterstown, Little Bellardine, Tullaghanstown, Togherstown and otherwise called Little Ballinlough, Lismachon, Clavanstown, Bellantry and Kenoristown, Berrelstown, Boltown and Faganstown otherwise Colledge Land in Molinan with all the Subdenominations thereof and all Woods, Underwoods and Appurtenances thereunto belonging all which said Lands and Premises are situate in the County of Meath and also All those four Houses now in the possession of Andrew Hyland, John Gillespy, the Representatives of Thomas Brennan deceased and the assignees of Thomas Collins respectively situate on the West side of Church Street in the County of the City of Dublin and also All that and those the yearly chief rent of One pound eighteen shillings and six pence payable out of the Lands of Tonlegeeth in the said County of Meath, The Yearly Chief Rent of One pound ten shillings payable out of the Lands of Glanidan and Ballynavin in the County of Westmeath, The yearly Chief Rent of One pound ten shillings payable out of the Lands of Martinstown and Carrick in the said County of Westmeath, The yearly Chief Rent of Three pounds fourteen shillings and three pence payable out of the Lands of Corstown and Baherkin and the yearly Chief Rent of Nine pence payable out of the Bog of Dunshaughlin in the said County of Meath and also all and singular other the Manors, Messuages, Towns, Lands and Premises of said Arthur James the Elder or any Person in trust for him have or hath any Estate of In heritance in possession or otherwise in the said Counties of Meath, Westmeath and County of the City of Dublin with their Appurtenances TO HAVE AND TO HOLD the said Lands and Premises and every part and parcel thereof with their and every of their rights Members and Appurtenances unto the said Randal Lord Baron Dunsany and Sir Robert Bellew their and each of their Executors Administrators and Assigns from the Day next before the Day of the date of these presents for and during and unto the full end and term of one whole year from thence next ensuing and fully to be completed and ended Yielding and Paying therefore unto the said Arthur James Plunkett the elder called Earl of Fingall his Heirs and Assigns the yearly rent of **one Pepper Corn** at the expiration of the said term if the same shall be lawfully demanded To the Intent and purpose that by virtue of these Presents and of the Statute for transferring uses into possession the said Lord Baron of Dunsany and Sir Robert Bellew may be in the actual Possession of the Premises and be thereby enabled to take and accept of a Grant and Release of the Freehold, reversion and Inheritance of the same premises and every part and parcel thereof to them the said Lord Baron of Dunsany and Sir Robert Bellew their and each of their Heirs and Assigns. IN WITNESS whereof the said James Plunkett the elder called Earl of Fingall and said Randal Lord Baron of Dunsany have hereunto respectively put their Titles of Honour and affixed their Seals and the said Sir Robert Bellew hath hereunto respectively put his Hand and Seal the Day and Year first above written.

Edward, 12th Baron of Dunsany, conformed in 1735 to the established Church in order, it is said, to save the Dunsany and Fingall property.

In *Seventy Years Young,* the Memories of Elizabeth, Countess of Fingall, she writes:
"The Dunsanys, having turned Protestant, were secure in their property, and, as in many cases, they became holders for their Catholic cousins of Killeen. That is to say that they swore that the Killeen property was theirs, holding it, every inch and every penny, in name. Each year Lord Dunsany had to swear afresh that the lands and property of Killeen were his."

7th EARL, ARTHUR JAMES, writes to Dr. P. J. Plunkett (Bishop of Meath)

KILLEEN CASTLE

10th January, 1791

'My Lord,

As it is uncertain, by your Lordship's obliging note to Lady Fingall, when we may have the pleasure of enjoying your Lordship's company, I am requested by Lord Dunsany to remit the enclosed note to your Lordship, since he is uncertain whether he may be at Dunsany, when your time may permit you to indulge us with your company, as he purposes shortly to go over to England or Scotland with his son. His Lordship mentioned nothing more than that he'd be obliged to me to have it delivered safe to you, which I promised him I would.

We were rejoiced to be assured that your Lordship was free from colds, and in perfect health. I imagine you are well informed how the Committee is going in Dublin. I every day wish there was more unanimity, and less pampheteering, as there is no doubt but advantage will be taken of the least dissension to prevent any further hope of relief from penal laws that are disgraceful to society; and what I dread will be the case if they continue to go on as they have done of late, and fear it has been brought on greatly by K's overzeal and contempt for many of the members who form the Committee.

Lady Fingall, Lady Theresa, and Mrs. Dease request to unite with me in best respects and sincerest wishes of the enjoyment of many many happy returns of the revolving seasons.

Believe me, with sincere regard and esteem, my Lord,

Your Lordship's most obedient, humble servant,

FINGALL'

ARTHUR JAMES, 8th Earl of Fingall, was born on the 9th September, 1759. (He succeeded his father to the Earldom on the 21st August, 1793.)

Frances, Countess of Fingall (1766-1835)

Miniature from a private collection

As Lord Killeen, he married on the 18th December, 1785, Frances, only daughter of John Donelan, Esq., of Bally Donelan, Co. Galway, and his wife Mabel Hore of Shannon, Co. Waterford. They were in France prior to the birth of their eldest son and moved to Switzerland in the wake of the French Revolution; their heir was born in Geneva. The Earl's brother, Luke, a Captain in the Austrian service, was killed in Italy in 1794. His brother William, Colonel in the Austrian service, died in 1806 in Prague.

The Earl and Countess had three children, Arthur James, Lady Harriet, and John, who died as an infant.

In 1795 he was readmitted to the House of Lords in Dublin; and the Earl was created a Justice of the Peace in 1803 as recorded in the ***Courier:***

'A very interesting correspondence has taken place in Dublin, between the Lord Chancellor Redesdale and Lord Fingall, the Premier Catholic Peer in Ireland. The correspondence arose out of the circumstances of Lord Fingall having been written to, requesting that he would be so good as to attend a meeting of the Magistrates, to take into consideration the state of the Country; to which his Lordship returned an answer, that he should have no objections, had he the honour of being a Magistrate; and as he was not, he was fearful that he might be considered an intruder. The Lord Lieutenant having been informed of the circumstances, with his accustomed propriety, directed that a Commission of the Peace should be made out and transmitted to Lord Fingall. The Lord Chancellor took the opportunity of sending a letter to his Lordship with the Commission of the Peace, complimenting him on his known loyalty and attachment to the King and Constitution, and touching on the subject of Catholicism. This produced a letter from Lord Fingall, equally complimentary, but referring his Lordship to the Catholic Clergy for information, which induced a continuation of the

correspondence in question, which had excited a considerable share of curiosity, and now occupies the conversation of all the high circles in the Irish Capital'.

On the 26th May, 1798, Lord Fingall lead his Catholic Yeomanry to fight the rebels on the Hill of Tara. He was Captain of the Skryne Cavalry and Yeomanry for a number of years.

Between 1803 and 1813 Killeen Castle underwent a massive structural change, with Francis Johnston drawing up the plans. Although it retained the old medieval structure, the additions extended the castle to twice its original size.

In 1812 the Earl, as the Premier Catholic Peer of Ireland, was to take the chair of the Catholic Committee, and was forcibly removed from it by a Police Magistrate, on the grounds that this Committee, to consider Catholic grievances and disabilities and petition for the removal of them, was an illegal assembly.

On the occasion of King George IV's visit to Ireland in 1821 he was made a Knight of St. Patrick, being the first Catholic to receive this honour. At this time Lord Byron refers to him in his biting satirical poem 'The Irish Avatar', which was aimed at the servility of the reception of the King by the Irish people. The lines alluding to the Earl of Fingall are:

'Wear, Fingall, thy trappings! O'Connell proclaim
His accomplishments! HIS!! and thy country convince.
Half an age's contempt was an error of fame
And that Hal is the rascaliest, sweetest young prince!
Will thy yard of blue riband, poor Fingall, recall
The fetters from millions of Catholic limbs?
Or, has it not bound thee the fastest of all
The slaves, who now hail their betrayer with hymns?'

(Byron's satire was proved misfounded with the granting of Catholic Emancipation in 1829.)

The Earl was made a Peer of the United Kingdom during the ministry of Earl Grey, by the patent dated 16th June, 1831, using the title Baron Fingall of Woolhampton Lodge, Bershire. He is reported to have voted in favour of reform of Parliament and supported the Whig ministers.

COURT JOURNAL, 1831

'The venerable Earl of Fingall appeared at the Levee on Wednesday, to kiss hands on receiving his English Peerage. His Majesty, whose courteous good nature is on all occasions so conspicuous, laid his particular injunctions on Lord Fingall not to kneel low, an amiable trait of kind attention in the Monarch. His Lordship was attended by his son, Lord Killeen, and Sir J. Dillon.'

The Earl was a Visitor and Trustee of the Royal College of Maynooth.

The Countess died in January, 1835, and the Earl on the 30th July, 1836, at his residence in Kingstown.

MAYNOOTH SEMINARY FOUNDED
1798 RISING IN WEXFORD, MEATH & ULSTER
FRENCH ARMY LANDS AT KILLALA
PRIMARY SCHOOL SYSTEM 1831
UNION OF BRITISH AND IRISH PARLIAMENTS
CATHOLIC EMANCIPATION
NAPOLEON-WATERLOO
ORANGE SOCIETY (ORDER) FOUNDED IN 1795

The Earl's insignia of the Order of St. Patrick

Richard By Divine Providence, Archbishop of Armagh, Primate and Metropolitan of all Ireland, also Judge or President of his Majesty's Court of Prerogative, for Causes Ecclesiastical and for Faculties in and throughout the whole Kingdom of Ireland, by Royal Authority rightly and lawfully constituted and established, TO our beloved in Christ, the Honourable Arthur James Plunkett commonly called Lord Baron Killeen and Frances Donelan of the Parish of Saint Mary in the City of Dublin Spinster ~ ~ ~

HEALTH in the Lord. WHEREAS, it is alledged you desire to proceed to the Solemnization of a true, pure and lawful Matrimony, WE being willing that these your honest Desires may the more speedily obtain due Effect, to the End, therefore, that this Marriage may be freely and lawfully solemnized in the Parish Church of Saint Mary ~ ~ aforesaid, or in any other decent and convenient Place, within the Kingdom of Ireland, by the Rector, Vicar or Curate, of the Parish of Saint Mary ~ aforesaid, or by any other Clerk, or Minister, rightly ordained, according to the Rites of the Church of Ireland, with Publication of Banns once only at the Time of the Solemnization of the said Marriage, at any Time of the Year or Day, PROVIDED there shall not appear any lawful Impediment in this Case, by Reason of Consanguinity, Affinity, Præcontract, or any other Cause whatever prohibited by Law, nor any Suit, Controversy, or Complaint be now moved or depending before any Judge, Ecclesiastical or Civil, for or by reason of any Marriage, contracted or alledged with either of you, WE, for lawful and reasonable Causes by US approved of, as far as in us lies, and the Laws of this Kingdom allow, dispense and freely grant our Licence and Faculty, as well to you the Parties contracting, as to the Rector, Vicar, or Curate of the said Parish of Saint Mary ~ ~ or to any other Clerk or Minister, rightly ordained, according to the Rites of the Church of Ireland, without Prejudice nevertheless to the Minister, where the said Woman is a Parishioner, to solemnize this Marriage between you, in the Manner above specified, according to the Form prescribed in the Book of Common Prayer, set forth for that Purpose by Authority of Parliament. AND WE likewise grant our Licence, in this Behalf, to all and every the faithful in Christ, who desire to be present at the Solemnization of the said Marriage; PROVIDED always, that if in this Case there shall hereafter appear any Fraud to have been committed at the Time of granting this Licence, either by false Suggestions or Concealment of the Truth, then this our Licence shall be void and of no Effect, to all Intents and Purposes of Law, as if the same had never been granted; and in that Case WE inhibit all Ministers whatever, if any thing of the Premisses shall come to their Knowledge, from proceeding to the Celebration of the said Marriage, without first consulting Us, or our Commissary. IN FAITH AND TESTIMONY whereof, We have caused the Seal of his Majesty's said Court of Prerogative to be affixed to these Presents. DATED the Eighteenth ~ ~ Day of December ~ ~ in the Year of our Lord One Thousand Seven Hundred and eighty five

Hen Upton
D Regr

Marriage Licence of Arthur James, 8th Earl of Fingall and Frances Donelan

8th EARL, ARTHUR JAMES, writes to Dr. P. J. Plunkett (Bishop of Meath)

9th May, 1795
Killeen Castle

'My dear Lord,

The uniform good wishes you have always been kind enough to express, and the friendly interest you have taken, since our first acquaintance, in every event that regarded this family, will not permit me to forego the pleasure of communicating to your Lordship that, on Thursday last, my claim to the title of Fingall, etc., was established by an unanimous resolution of the House of Lords. This business had been put off on Monday, the day first appointed, as many of the peers, I hope from their inclination to hear liberality, though, unfortunately not to see it prevail, were that day taken up attending the Catholic question in the Commons.

Your Lordship will readily conceive that I must find no small source for anxiety now removed; indeed the only alloy to my present satisfaction is the reflection that all those to whom this event would have been both so flattering and agreeable were not permitted to see the time to its completion. But they, I hope, enjoy a happiness which neither the honours or advantages of this life are to be compared with. It is as fruitless to repine, as to wish to recall them. But one beneficial lesson is, I hope, strongly impressed on my mind, by the recollection of that person who so long and ardently wished to see his family restored to its native country, by being replaced in its former situation-a firm resolution never to deviate from those principles he so eminently possessed, which, in our name, have, in most instances, been so religiously adhered to, and by a continuation of which we shall, I hope, ever deserve credit in the eyes of those whose good opinion is worth looking up to. Could anything enhance the value of the boon conferred on me, the handsome manner in which the whole pursuit was attended by those who officially were concerned, must add to the value of the acquisition.

There was a most numerous attendance of peers. The conduct of the Chancellor was, in the general opinion, more that of an advocate than of a judge, though, as your Lordship knows, this was by me both unsought and almost unexpected. There were at least sixteen of your confreres, with the Archbishops of Dublin and Cashel, competing who should cry content most forcibly on the admission of a Papist, at least to the right of becoming a member of their house. The time is not, I hope, remote when that restriction which impedes the full enjoyment of every privilege will, with the same unanimity, be conceded. At all events, my object is now completely attained, and I trust by no other means than such as reflect credit on the Government, and no disgrace on the individual.

I have left Lady Fingall in town, whither I return on Monday. Our youngest child has been very ill. We shall, I hope, soon become inhabitants of this old castle, to which, I trust, it is needless of me to say, Your Lordship's visits are ever truly welcome. I left my mother very well yesterday.

I have the honour to be, my dear Lord,
Your very faithful and most obedient servant,

FINGALL'

ARTHUR JAMES, 9th Earl of Fingall, was born in Geneva on the 29th March, 1791. He married Louisa Emilia Corbally on the 11th December, 1817.

> *'She was the only daughter of Elias Corbally, Esq., of Corbalton Hall, County of Meath, in which county his family is possessed of an extensive landed property. Matthew E. Corbally, Esq., her ladyship's brother, represents that county in the Imperial Parliament.'*

They had six sons and two daughters, Arthur James, Lord Killeen; Elias Robert who died shortly after his 21st birthday; William Matthew, who, after serving as an officer in the 23rd Welsh Fusiliers, joined the Redemptorists in 1850 and was the first Irish man to join the Order; Edmund Luke worked at Her Majesty's Treasury, Whitehall, London; George John, barrister-at-law; Francis Richard, international diplomat, Ambassador at Vienna - 1900/1905; Emma Frances; and Henrietta.

> *'The Earl represented the County of Meath [House of Commons] in the Liberal interest in the first three Parliaments of the Reign of William IV as Lord Killeen, and succeeded to the family honours on July 30th, 1836. His Lordship was for many years Lord Lieutenant and Custos Rotulorum of Meath and a Guardian and Visitor of the College of St. Patrick, Maynooth. He became a Peace Commissioner in Ireland in 1834, and a Knight of St. Patrick in 1846. He was one of the leading political Catholics, and was always regarded as of the moderate Catholic party who adhered to Whig principles. He was also a Privy Councellor.'*

During Lord Melbourne's administration he was a lord-in-waiting to the Queen and, with the Countess, attended Queen Victoria's coronation.

In 1839 he became the first Chairman of the Work House in Dunshaughlin and was also a Guardian.

Killeen Castle itself had been considerably enlarged by the 8th Earl in the early 1800s. The 9th Earl extended it further in 1841, under the architect James Shiel, and changed the entrance from the west to the east façade. The design is thought to have been influenced by Windsor Castle.

In the primary valuation carried out between 1848 and 1865, the Earl of Fingall is listed ... Castle, Offices & Land ... 904 acres ... total valuation of property £1,100. Also there were 51 acres at Clowanstown. A further 33 properties and farms, of various sizes, were leased by the Earl.

The Earl died suddenly at his residence 47, Montague Square, London, on the 21st April, 1869, his wife having died at Brighton on the 7th April, 1866.

1838 DICKENS PUBLISHED *OLIVER TWIST*
GREAT FAMINE IN IRELAND
1848 RISING IN MUNSTER
1849 QUEEN VICTORIA VISITS IRELAND
LANDLORD-TENANT PROBLEMS
FLORENCE NIGHTINGALE - CRIMEAN WAR
UNIFICATION OF ITALY

"Work in progress" on restoration of plaque on north side of castle. Erected by 9th Earl of Fingall.

© Fitz.Gerald & Associates Architects

CASTELLUM HOC
This Castle
EXTRUCTUM
Built
ANNO DOMINI 1181
The year of our Lord 1181
AMPLIAVIT
Extended (made it more ample)
ALTITUDINE AUXIT
Increased in Height
ET ORNAVIT
And adorned and beautified
ARTURUS JACOBUS
Arthur James
BARO DE KILLEEN
Baron of Killeen
OCTODECIMUS
Eighteenth
COMES VERO NONUS DE
Ninth Earl of
FINGALL
ANNO DOMINI 1839
Year of our Lord 1839
JACOBUS SHIEL ARCHITECTUS
James Shiel Architect

9th EARL, ARTHUR JAMES (whilst Lord Killeen), writes to Dr. P. J. Plunkett (Bishop of Meath)

Dublin, November 25th, 1820

'My dear Lord,

This day's post has brought me your Lordship's very kind congratulations on the addition of a son to my family; congratulations than which none can be to me more valuable because I am convinced none can be to me more sincere. Allow me, my dear Lord, to express how sensibly we all feel this kind mark of your Lordship's attention, and how much I personally owe to the person who, under divine providence, was the instrument of procuring me as much happiness and as much unalloyed bliss as is to be hoped for in this world. To your Lordship both our families feel that they are indebted for a considerable share of the felicity which has hitherto blessed our union, and they feel convinced that no one more sincerely desires its long continuance than your Lordship. You will be glad to hear that Lady Killeen and her son continue as well as possible. The young gentleman is to be baptised on Monday. Dr. Troy has promised to perform the ceremony, and I expect Mr. Corbally in town, who, with my mother, is to be a sponsor. He is to be named Elias Robert.

Allow me to reiterate to your Lordship the united thanks of the families for your very warm and sincere felicitations, and believe me to be, my dear Lord,

With the greatest regard and esteem

Your Lordship's faithful and obliged servant,

KILLEEN'

9th EARL, ARTHUR JAMES (whilst Lord Killeen) writes to Dr. P. J. Plunkett (Bishop of Meath)

'My dear Lord,

On my return from Dublin, Lady Killeen delivered to me your Lordship's kind invitation to dinner at your hospitable table on Sunday next. It would have given me great pleasure to have had the honour of waiting upon you, and also to have met Mr. O'Connell, but Mr. Corbally expects some of the grand jurors here on their way to the assizes, and we are obliged to be in Trim so early on Monday that it will not be in my power to accept of your Lordship's very polite invitation.

I have the honour to be,

Your Lordship's very faithful
and obedient servant,

KILLEEN'

Corbalton, 8th March, 1824

Arthur James, 9th Earl of Fingall	Hon. Sir Francis Plunkett, Ambassador Vienna, 1900-5	Countess of Fingall	Hon. George Plunkett, Barrister at Law	Hon. William Plunkett, Redemptorist

Silhouette of 9th Earl, his wife and three of his sons.
© Major and Mrs. J. Kirk.

Pastel of a son of the 9th Earl of Fingall

Engraving of Countess of Fingall. Published in London, dated May 1842
© Lord & Lady Dunsany 2008

Titled: Earl of Fingall
Dated: 14th November 1861

Titled: Lady Fingall
Dated: 20th February 1861

Titled: Lady Fingall
Dated: 3rd November 1860

Titled: Hon. E. Plunkett
Dated: 20th February 1861

Titled: Hon. & Rev. William Plunkett
Dated: 14th September 1861

Titled: Hon. George Plunkett
Dated: 8th April 1861

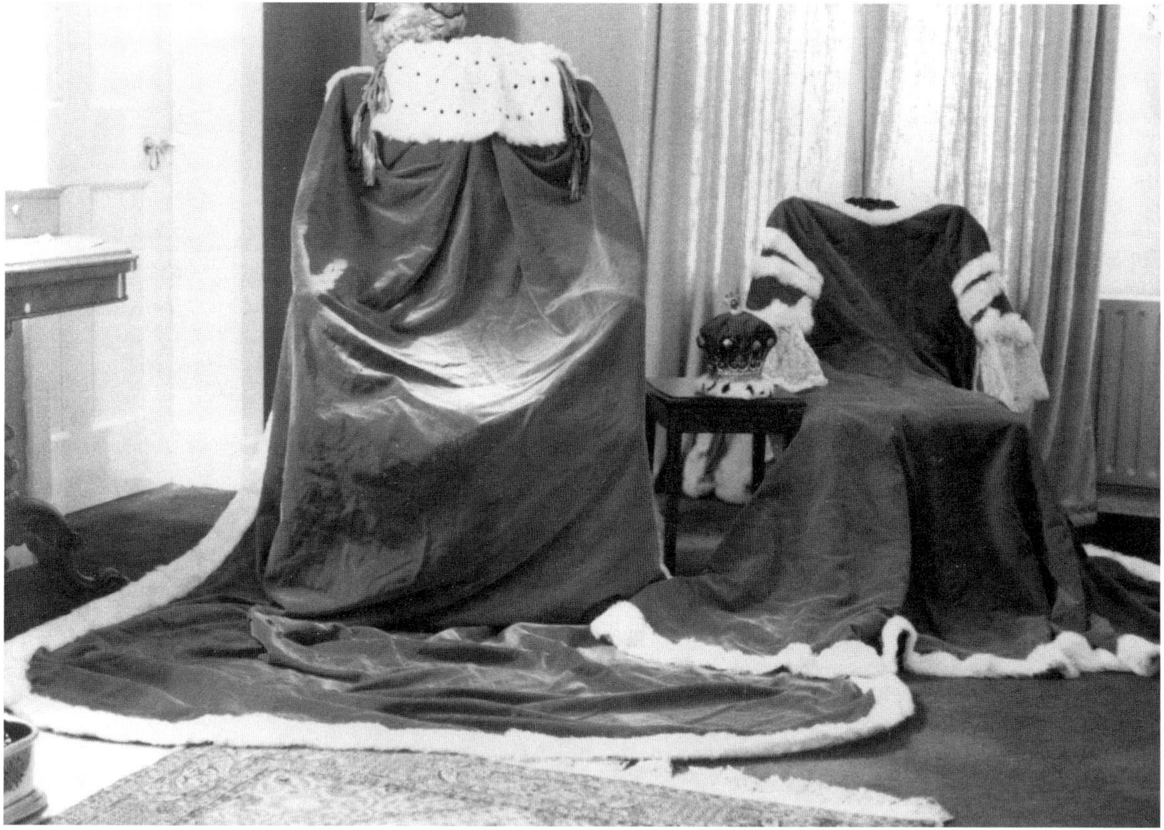

The robes worn by the 9th Earl and Countess at Queen Victoria's Coronation

1985 Paul Tierney

ARTHUR JAMES, 10th Earl of Fingall, was born in Naples on 10th May, 1819. He was a Major in the 8th Hussars and married Elise (Elizabeth) Mary, elder daughter of Monsieur Francis Alexis and Apolonia Rio (née Jones) of the City of Paris, on the 12th February, 1857. Elise Mary's father was a Chevalier of the Legion of Honour and her mother Welsh. They had three children - Arthur James, Mary Louisa and Henrietta Marie.

The Countess died of consumption near Pau, France, 25th November, 1862, and the Earl continued to live in France. He moved his young family to Paris where they received their education and, although he inherited the Earldom on the 22nd April, 1869, did not return to Ireland, and Killeen, until 1880.

On his arrival 'home' he was presented with a beautiful hand-illuminated address by subscribers from the locality.

The Earl died on the 24th April, 1881, and was buried in Killeen.

SECRET BALLOT ACT
HOME RULE MOVEMENT
LAND LEAGUE, CAPTAIN BOYCOTT
GERMANY UNITED
ALEXANDER II OF RUSSIA ASSASSINATED

ADDRESS BY PEOPLE OF KILLEEN/DUNSANY TO THE RIGHT HON. THE EARL OF FINGALL (TENTH EARL)

My Lord, on behalf of your Tenants, and of many who have ever shared in their warmest feelings for your noble House, we approach your Lordship to congratulate you on your return to Ireland.

Long have we deplored your absence from your ancestral house, the regret which moved us as we looked on the untenanted lordly castle of Killeen, was deepened into sorrow beyond expression by the cause that compelled you to withdraw from the house you loved. Protracted illness had imposed that necessity upon you and to this sacrifice, which deprived us of many advantages, we were resigned, in the hope that a more genial climate might restore you to health and vigour. The result has largely corresponded to our wishes and anticipations and we are solaced at finding you once more in the midst of a people by whom you are revered and beloved.

By your presence amongst us the most cherished memories of your illustrious House are revived. We cannot fail to recall on this happy occasion the rare examples of exalted rank united with christian humility; of heroic virtue tried in fiery ordeal; of singular loyalty to an oppressed Creed; of high born unselfish patriotism; of kindly sympathy with distress; which your Noble house has given to history as precious records, and to a nation for a heritage beyond price.

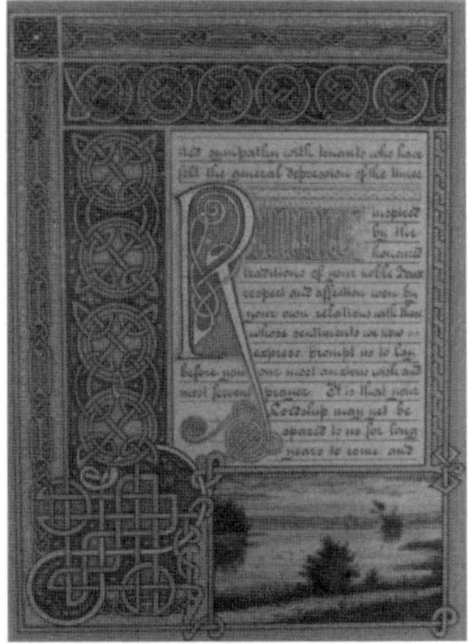

Of the happy relations which have always been maintained between the tenants and the proprietors of the Fingall Estates, we can speak with pride in these evil days when all around is heard an angry strife of conflicting interests. No grievances disquiet those who, as occupiers of the soil, are fortunate enough to hold it on such equitable terms as the Noble Lords of Fingall have been satisfied to impose. We gratefully record your first act as Landlord to have been a remission, in several instances, of arrears, and your latest, a substantial abatement of moderate rents, in unsolicited sympathy with tenants who have felt the general depression of the times.

Reverence, inspired by the honoured traditions of your noble house, respect and affection won by your own relations with those whose sentiments we now express, prompt us to lay before you our most anxious wish and most fervent prayer. It is that your Lordship may yet be spared to us for long years to come, and that every fond hope of a father's heart may be blessed in the fulfilment with regard to those dear children who are your most sacred treasure and are, with you, our most assured pledges that in the future, as in the past, the good old ties which connect the Fingall Tenants with the Lord of the Soil may not be severed.

Signed on behalf of the subscribers

R.A. Donaldson	Chairman
Nicholas R. Logan	Treasurer
David Morrissy	Hon. Sec.

July, 1880

ARTHUR JAMES FRANCIS, 11th Earl of Fingall, was born in Rome on the 1st April, 1859. He grew up in France, spending much of his time after his mother's death, in Paris with his father and two sisters. Occasionally, he visited Killeen for hunting in the winter holidays and lived by himself, with a couple of servants, in the big house. Lord Killeen eventually persuaded his father to return to Ireland and the Fingall Family were back in residence for his 21st birthday.

'The butler, preparing the great celebrations, got gloriously drunk and set the dining-room on fire, damaging the only good pictures at Killeen, including two van Dycks of King Charles I and Queen Henrietta Maria.'

The 11th Earl inherited on the 24th April, 1881, at the age of twenty-two and, the same year, was High Sheriff of Meath. He was State Steward to the Lord Lieutenant of Ireland 1882-1885.

On the 15th May, 1883, Arthur James Francis married Elizabeth Mary, daughter of Mr. George Burke, J. P., of Danesfield, Co. Galway, in the Archbishop of Dublin's Private Chapel in Rutland Square, Dublin. The Countess was only seventeen

There are two editorials dated 1885, sources unknown, referring to the Earl and Countess.

'His lordship is the representative of one of the oldest Catholic families in Meath. He lived chiefly abroad with his noble father until shortly before the latter's death at Killeen, when the present peer determined to reside at the family seat in Meath. Here he commenced immediately to show those many good qualities which stamp the true country gentleman, and which have endeared him to all with whom he is acquainted. Passionately fond of horses, his first care upon going to Meath was to get together a stud of the right sort, and very soon he showed well to the front by riding a good second in the Empress's Cup at the Meath Sportman's Races the first season Her Imperial Majesty, the Empress of Austria, hunted in Ireland. As a landlord Lord Fingall is one of the few exceptions of that much-maligned class in the Sister Isle, being very popular with his tenants. Living in their midst, knowing their wants, and spending his money freely among them, they look up to him as their friend and advisor, and he has never had any difficulty in collecting rents on the Fingall Property.

As a sportsman Lord Fingall may be described as thorough in every sense of the word. He is a staunch preserver of foxes, and a liberal supporter of the county hounds, as well as a leading man and manager of the neighbouring "Wards". Besides being an officer in the 5th Battalion, Prince of Wales Leinster Regiment (Royal Canadians), his lordship filled the honourable post of State Steward in the household of Earl Spencer, when the latter was Viceroy of Ireland.'

'The Countess of Fingall is the eldest surviving daughter of Mr. George Burke, J.P., of Danesfield, County Galway. Taken away from Ireland in her childhood by her parents, owing to their sad bereavement of two children with a few weeks, Miss Burke was educated on the continent and in England, and did not revisit her native land until she went back to it nearly a grown woman, "Made to engage all hearts, and charm all eyes". Her reign in Dublin society as Miss Burke was, as might be expected, extremely short, for in May, 1883, she married the youthful Earl of Fingall. Her ladyship is one of the fairest ornaments of the Viceregal Court, where her noble husband fills with so much ability the high and important office of State Steward; but nowhere is she seen to such advantage as at home - as the hospitable and kindly mistress of Killeen Castle.'

The Earl and Countess had four children, Oliver James Horace, Lord Killeen, Gerald William Desmond, Mary Elizabeth and Henrietta Maria. Lord Fingall was in Australia in 1896, served in South Africa 1900-1901 (Boer War), was Master of the Horse in 1905 and took part in the First World War.

While the Earl loved the peace and tranquillity of Killeen and was content with his hunting, tending to his horses and meeting his tenants, the Countess was the opposite. She too, in her own way, loved Killeen, but also thrived on an active social life, spending much of her time away from the family home, visiting friends and acquaintances. Lady Fingall mixed with many of the great figures of the late Victorian and Edwardian era, both in Ireland and across the Irish Sea.

During the life of the Earl the Gladstone Land Act of 1881, which established the Land Commission, was passed. The Wyndham Act of 1903 and the subsequent consolidating Land Act of 1923, in the initial years of the Free State, set in motion the machinery whereby much of the Fingall land was vested in its tenant farmer occupiers.

The Earl and Countess were staunch supporters of Horace Plunkett in the establishment of the Agricultural Co-Operative Movement in Ireland, and in his endeavours in pursuit of his slogan 'better farming, better business, better living' for all in Irish agriculture. (They even planted tobacco in their garden and apple trees in the paddock!) Horace enlisted the help of the Countess in setting up the United Irishwomen's Association in 1910, which was the forerunner of the present Irish Countrywomen's Association. Together, the Earl and Countess provided Horace, a bachelor, with a domestic and family background for social activities in pursuit of his objectives.

The remaining family property at Upper Woolhampton, Berkshire, was sold in 1913 to the English Benedictine Fathers of the Family of Douai to be used for 'Scholastic and Monastic' purposes.

The deed disentailing the estate was executed on 22nd November, 1918. Lands and residences were sold at Berrillstown, Glebe, Killeen (Lough Lawrence Division) and Clavanstown/Clowanstown but the Earl's directive 'not to sell any of the property which is in direct line of view from Killeen Castle' was adhered to.

The Earl died suddenly on the 12th November, 1929, and his son, Oliver James Horace, became the 12th, and last, Earl of Fingall.

It was almost as though the eventual passing of Killeen Castle and demesne from the Plunkett Family had been foreseen, with Elizabeth, Countess of Fingall, remarking 'what a lovely ruin it would make'; and Horace Plunkett writing 'it stands as the monument of an order which has passed and awaits the passing to a religious order, which will continue its chill; its evacuation and quick ruin or most likely, the sporting multi-millionaire from America'.

The Countess of Fingall died in Dublin on Saturday, 28th October, 1944, and was laid to rest in the old manorial church at Killeen. She left, as a legacy to future generations, an insight into her life and times in the book *Seventy Years Young, Memories of Elizabeth, Countess of Fingall.*

WORLD WAR I
IRISH INDEPENDENCE
LAND ACTS

11th Earl as a four year old

Elizabeth
Countess Fingall

Arthur James Francis,
11th Earl

OLIVER JAMES HORACE PLUNKETT, 12th Earl of Fingall, was born on the 17th June, 1896, at South Audley Street, London, where his mother was residing at that time. His father was in Australia gold-mining with Lord Casey (Governor General of Australia).

The family returned to Killeen and one of the first recollections Oliver James had was of his father returning from the Boer War. The Earl had been driven by wagonette to Killeen Gate, from there the local men pulled the wagonette to the front door of the castle; Lord Killeen, as he was then, followed on a donkey. He was five years of age. The Earl's safe return was greeted with many celebrations.

Much of Lord Killeen's early years were spent in the nurseries with his brother and two sisters. Mrs. Wall was his nurse when he was very young, later Mrs. Keogh. Miss Croft was the governess. There were 132 steps from the nurseries to the kitchen and Oliver James had fond memories of Mrs. Peacock, who made beautiful rissoles!

His main recreations, as a child, were gardening and riding. Laurence Mahon was the gardener and quite a strict taskmaster. After riding, the Fingall children were expected to clean their tack and see to their animals. Another favourite pastime was roller-skating around the flagstone floor in the kitchen area - there was about a quarter of an acre.

His mother was away a lot and he saw her approximately once a fortnight. However, her sister, Florence Burke, was often at Killeen (she became Lady Geary) and used to read to the children. She was like a mother to the Killeen children.

In 1906, at the age of ten, Lord Killeen was sent to preparatory school, St. Anthony's in Eastbourne, Sussex. Whilst home in Ireland in 1907, dressed in white satin breeches and shirt, he acted as pageboy to King Edward VII when the King, over for the International Exhibition, entertained in the Viceregal Lodge in the Phoenix Park.

Lord Killeen moved on to Downside, near Bath, in 1910. (Saint Oliver Plunkett's body was laid to rest in the Benedictine Abbey of St. Gregory the Great at Downside in 1883.) He enjoyed school and was keen on games, particularly cricket and rugby. On one memorable occasion he took all ten wickets against Kingswood School.

From Downside he went to Sandhurst in 1914 for approximately one year and joined the 17th Lancers in August, 1914. His father wished he had joined the 8th Hussars and followed family tradition. From Sandhurst he went to the Curragh.

In 1915 Lord Killeen went to France and to war. General Haig was his Commanding Officer. He was wounded during 1916 and spent nearly a year in hospital while his leg healed. After convalescing in Ireland he went back to France. He was mostly on The Somme - returning to Ireland when he had leave. He was awarded the Military Cross.

After the 1914-1918 War, Lord Killeen was posted with the 17th Lancers to Cologne, for about a year, and raced a little in Beligum and Germany. Then back to England and barracks in Bulford, followed by a posting to Germany as A.D.C. to General Morland

Jessica, Countess of Fingall, at the time of her marriage.

Lord Killeen met his first wife, Jessica, daughter of Alan Hughes of Allerford, Somerset, England, just after the War during the hunting season in Ireland. Shortly after, he won his first race (20th August, 1920) on a horse called 'Anytime', and from then on rode pretty regularly. In 1926 he marrried Jessica.

Lord Killeen considered 'his chief triumph' a horse called 'Gib', bought for £30 in 1923. Not broken until he was a four-year-old, Gib was sent to trainer Percy Woodland, and after winning twice in 1928 went on to win six races off the reel. Gib was sold prior to Oliver's posting to Egypt.

On the 12th November, 1929, the 11th Earl died and the 12th Earl inherited Killeen Castle and over 1,000 acres. Whilst in London, after his father's death, he exercised his prerogative and attended the House of Lords once or twice but never spoke.

In 1930 the Earl completed an unforgettable treble in the annals of National Hunt Racing for Jack Anthony, by winning the National Hunt Steeplechase on Sir Lindsay, the trainer having already won the Gold Cup and the Champion Hurdle. On the 3rd October that year, he was sent to Egypt with the 17th Lancers and returned the 21st March, 1931, arriving in Ireland in May, 1931, and, whilst alterations were being carried out at Killeen Castle, lived for a short time at Corbalton Hall and then Grange. The Earl and Countess moved back into Killeen on the 13th July, 1931.

The Earl was appointed Steward of the National Hunt in 1931. He served five periods - a record - two before World War II and three after. He was also Joint Master of the Ward Hounds and on the original Board of the National Stud.

Oliver, Earl of Fingall, served in the army again between 1934-1945 this time doing military duty in England.

In 1947 the Earl crossed the Atlantic and judged at Madison Square, New York, and at the Winter Fair in Toronto, Canada. It was an experience he very much enjoyed. Most years he and his wife managed two trips to France.

In 1951 the Earl sold Killeen to Sir Victor Sassoon and, at Sassoon's request, he remained as manager. The Earl and Countess stayed at Killeen Castle for a further two years.

Sir Victor ran a stud farm from Killeen (he never lived there). He sold Killeen in 1963.

Lord Fingall owned many good horses - Gib, Roddy Owen, No Other, Why, Tother, Honorable Aura, Another Girl and Baldoyle. With Roddy Owen he won the Cheltenham Gold Cup in 1959. Horses were his life, and he found their feats easier to recall than those of his ancestors.

The Earl of Fingall's racing colours were white, green with white hooped sleeve, and green cap.

After finally moving from Killeen Castle, Lord and Lady Fingall lived at Corballis. Jessica died on the 14th April, 1965. Her funeral service was in the parish church of St. Seachnall's (Church of Ireland), Dunshaughlin, Co. Meath and she was buried in the adjoining graveyard.

> *'The sad news of the recent death of Jessica Fingall in Dublin will have caused great grief to her many old friends on and around Exmoor. The daughter of Mr. and Mrs. Allan Hughes, of Lynch, and the younger sister of Lady Pilcher, she was a keen staghunter as a young woman and during the First World War she was the Master and Joint Master with Miss Aston of the Quarme Harriers.*
>
> *After her marriage to Lord Killeen (as he was then) in 1926 she made her home with him in Ireland, but frequently visited her mother and sister at Lynch paying her last visit there only a week or so before she died.*
>
> *Her many old friends on Exmoor and in Ireland will remember her as a woman of great courage, gifted with a remarkable sense of humour and a very ready wit. These qualities made her a stimulating companion and a great favourite in any company.'*

After her death, the Earl took a trip to Australia. During the course of his sojourn in Australia he visited the widow of his life-long friend Frank Evan Richardson, whom he had first met at the outbreak of World War I. Subsequently, Clair Hilda Richardson (*née* Salmon) and the Earl of Fingall were married at Brompton Oratory, London, on the 4th May, 1966. Father Tucker officiated. After the wedding they paid a lengthy visit to Australia. They returned to Corballis whilst their house at The Commons was being built. The work involved was mainly supervised by the Countess, who took a great interest in every aspect of their new home and created a beautiful garden. It was ready in May, 1968.

During his riding years, Lord Fingall was easy to distinguish as he always wore glasses. It was said of him that 'he was as blind as a bat and brave as a lion'. He was regarded by all who knew him as 'a lovely man', a gentleman, who was never known to let anyone down, and endowed with a wonderful sense of fun and wit. He lived very simply, except when on holiday - then the best of everything was not good enough!

In October, 1975, the Earl and Countess attended the Canonisation of Saint Oliver Plunkett; the Earl presented a candle to the Pope during the Offertory Procession. Afterwards they lunched at the Irish College, as guests of Cardinal Conway, and had an audience with the Pope, who presented them with a medallion and rosary.

Lord Fingall had many falls during his racing years from which he successfully recovered but on the 29th December, 1978, he slipped and fractured his femur and pelvis and, thereafter, was mostly confined to a wheelchair. He found the inactivity hard to bear after such an active life and, after heart failure, died in Navan Hospital at 7.30 p.m. on the 5th March, 1984. He was buried on Wednesday, 7th March, at Dunsany Church, which was his wish; thus the last of the line, 21st Baron Killeen, 12th Earl of Fingall, Premier Catholic Peer of Ireland, Oliver James Horace Plunkett was laid to rest.

At the Memorial Service on the 29th March the oration ended: 'He walked with Kings but kept the common touch'.

Clair, Countess of Fingall
Circa 1993

Clair, Countess of Fingall, M.B.E., sold her much-loved home - The Commons - and retired to Australia in 1985, where she was surrounded by family but still kept her ties with Ireland.

Clair had celebrated her 99th birthday shortly before her death on 14th March, 2002. Her Memorial Service was held on 26th April, 2002 at All Saints' Anglican Church, in Geelong, Victoria, where she is buried.

ECONOMIC WAR WITH BRITAIN
WORLD WAR II - FIRST ATOMIC BOMB
GANDHI IN INDIA - INDEPENDENCE
KOREAN WAR

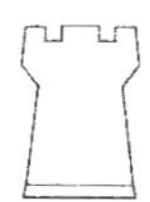

The Earl and Countess of Fingall at Ascot Races
© Major and Mrs. J. Kirk *Circa 1930*

The 12th Earl on his favourite horse, Annie Circa 1955

The Great Porch.
© Clair, Countess of Fingall

Circa 1950

Entrance from Porch to Oak Hall
© Clair, Countess of Fingall

Circa 1950

Picture Gallery - West Side
© Clair, Countess of Fingall

Circa 1950

Grand Staircase

© Clair, Countess of Fingall

Circa 1950

Close up of Grand Staircase with Quatrefoil Motif
© Clair, Countess of Fingall

Circa 1950

Dining Room
© Clair, Countess of Fingall

Circa 1950

Dining Room
© Clair, Countess of Fingall

Circa 1950

Library (St. Oliver Plunkett's vestments in glass cabinet)
© Clair, Countess of Fingall

Circa 1950

Library
© Clair, Countess of Fingall

Circa 1950

Library
© Clair, Countess of Fingall

Circa 1950

The Oak Hall

The White Bedroom

Irish Tatler & Sketch (October 1950)

The Stable Yard
© Clair, Countess of Fingall Circa 1950

Grazing in the shadow of Killeen Castle
© Clair, Countess of Fingall Circa 1950

A portion of the Walled Garden
© Clair, Countess of Fingall

Circa 1950

KILLEEN CASTLE

Killeen Castle was built in 1181 by Hugh de Lacy. The early castle may have consisted of a series of strong towers, with a walled enclosure (bailey), where the great hall and kitchens were situated. From the initial structure a fine medieval tower house developed, gracing the 'lordship of Killeen'. Nearby, a village grew up and markets were held in the vicinity of the castle. The road from Dunshaughlin ran through Killeen, crossing Tara, and heading north and, at this time, the Plunkett/Cruise Memorial was a wayside cross. Another road went to Trim, then the capital of Meath crossing Killeen and Dunsany and the two Pale castles (Killeen Castle and Dunsany Castle) guarded these roads. (Most of North Leinster was known as 'Plunkett Country'.)

From the late seventeenth to the late eighteenth centuries Killeen Castle became dilapidated, due possibly to the enforced absences of the Earls. Not until the time of the 7th Earl of Fingall was an attempt made to make the castle habitable once again. This was in the late 1770s and, with the restoration of the castle, it is likely that the demesne was landscaped, the lake and decoy added.

The earliest representation of Killeen shows the castle as it looked in the 1780s, having been restored by the 7th Earl. The architect, Francis Johnston, was engaged by the 8th Earl to draw plans to modernise the castle. Thomas Wogan Browne, of Clongowes Wood, Co. Kildare, an amateur architect, acted as advisor to the Earl. Many plans and ideas were considered before work commenced in 1803, continuing to 1813 when the building was completed. In the lifetime of the 9th Earl, James Shiel was engaged to extend Killeen and he considerably altered Johnston's work. At that time, the entrance was moved to the east façade (the rere of Johnston's castle). The 'tough old fortress' almost disappeared - internally it is easier to identify the 'old' and 'new' parts of the castle, the thickness of the walls (five feet) revealing their age. The twin towers at the front of the castle bear the dates H:II 1181 and V:I 1841. The building was reputed, locally, to have 365 windows (one for every day of the year).

The Stable Yard, where the 11th and 12th Earls spent much of their time, lay to the North East. Close by lay the extensive walled gardens.

In 1941, the Wedding Scenes from the film version of Daphne Du Maurier's novel *Hungry Hill* were shot at Killeen.

Killeen Castle was sold in 1951 to Sir Victor Sassoon, who ran it as a stud farm, with the Earl as manager. At the time the 12th Earl finally moved from the castle, in July 1953, there was a large auction, lasting six days, of the 'entire valuable contents'.

Sir Victor sold Killeen in 1963 to Daniel Wildenstein, a wealthy American, and thus ended the 'Fingall' association with Killeen. Part of the James Bond movie *Casino Royale* with David Niven and Deborah Kerr was shot at the castle in 1966.

In 1978 Killeen changed hands again, and was purchased by Basil Brindley from the world of advertising, who continued to run it as a stud farm.

On Saturday, the 16th May, 1981, Killeen Castle was set on fire maliciously. Petrol had been poured on the wooden staircase and floorboards in the central portion of the castle and the fire caused extensive damage.

In December 1989, Killeen was once again sold. Snowbury Limited purchased Killeen Castle and Estate from Christopher Slattery in 1995 and, whilst planning and design work were underway, continued the long tradition of operating a Stud Farm.

Following completion of the planning process, work commenced on the restoration of the castle in January, 2005. Stonework, turrets, towers, family crests and battlements have been meticulously restored. The west tower will continue to provide access to a viewing platform. The castle acquired a new roof, using slates from the old hunter's yard and imported salvage slates. There were 172 windows and, of these, 166 were reinstated. The remaining six window openings will be utilised to link into the proposed five star hotel which will be built on the north side of the castle.

The estate, which comprises nearly 600 acres, is undergoing major changes. An 18 hole Jack Nicklaus Signature championship golf course now surrounds the castle. The Cruise-Plunkett fifteenth century wayside cross overlooks the first and eighteenth fairways, and the course incorporates a number of new lakes to punish any errant shot! Majestic old trees within the demesne have been retained and these have been complemented by new plantings of thousands of mature trees and shrubs. Native species such as oak, ash, beech have been utilised where appropriate. These replacement plantings were sourced from Northern Germany due to the compatibility of the climatic conditions. The overall landscaping renewal is the largest undertaken in Ireland in recent years. An impressive Club House and Golf Academy complete the complex. Killeen Castle Golf Course will host the Solheim Cup in 2011.

Great attention is being given to detail and old and new are being subtly integrated. The castle gardens have been reinstated and, nearby, a nineteenth century arched servants' underpass is being restored. The facing of the castle lake, through which the Rock River runs, has been repaired and a pontoon bridge built out over the lake to provide a fishing platform and a vantage point to view Lady's Well.

As part of the overall plan for the estate over one hundred and fifty new dwellings are being built. Elegant lodges, detached houses and two courtyard complexes are being carefully interspersed around the estate.

And so begins a new chapter in the history of Killeen Castle.

The altar from the private oratory in Killeen Castle was presented by the Fingall Family to the Church of the Assumption, Dunsany, when the present church was built 1893/94.

Archaeology

Before the commencement of an extensive building programme, coupled with golf course development, within Killeen Castle demesne, an archaeological programme was put in place under the auspices of Margaret Gowan & Co. Ltd., financed by Snowbury Ltd. Three initial testing programmes had already been carried out before the major dig began in January 2005, headed by Christine Baker, M.A. This work concluded in April, 2006.

The excavations proved to be extensive and rewarding, surpassing all expectation. Eight major sites were identified. The sites varied from late Neolithic/early Bronze Age to Anglo-Norman and Medieval periods. Disturbance by nineteenth-century agricultural activity and construction was also encountered. Various kilns, a probable ringfort, burial grounds and ancient roads were located. Artefacts include a probable prehistoric hollow scraper, numerous sherds of twelfth to fourteenth-century pottery, a fifteenth-century key and a silver penny (1280/1300) from the reign of Edward I.

The layout of the golf course was redesigned to allow for the preservation in situ of the majority of the sites.

15th Century Key found at Killeen
© John Sunderland (Courtesy of Margaret Gowen & Co. Ltd.)

IMAGES OF KILLEEN CASTLE

The original castle
(by kind permission of the Irish Architectural Archive).

The Medieval Tower House was a three-storey, four-bay façade, with a massive crenellated parapet. Onto this at the NW corner (to the left) a small single-storey private oratory was added, and this was balanced by a similar projection on the opposite corner. From the hall a wide staircase led to each floor above, each storey containing a large chamber, which could be subdivided. The flanking towers contained small chambers.

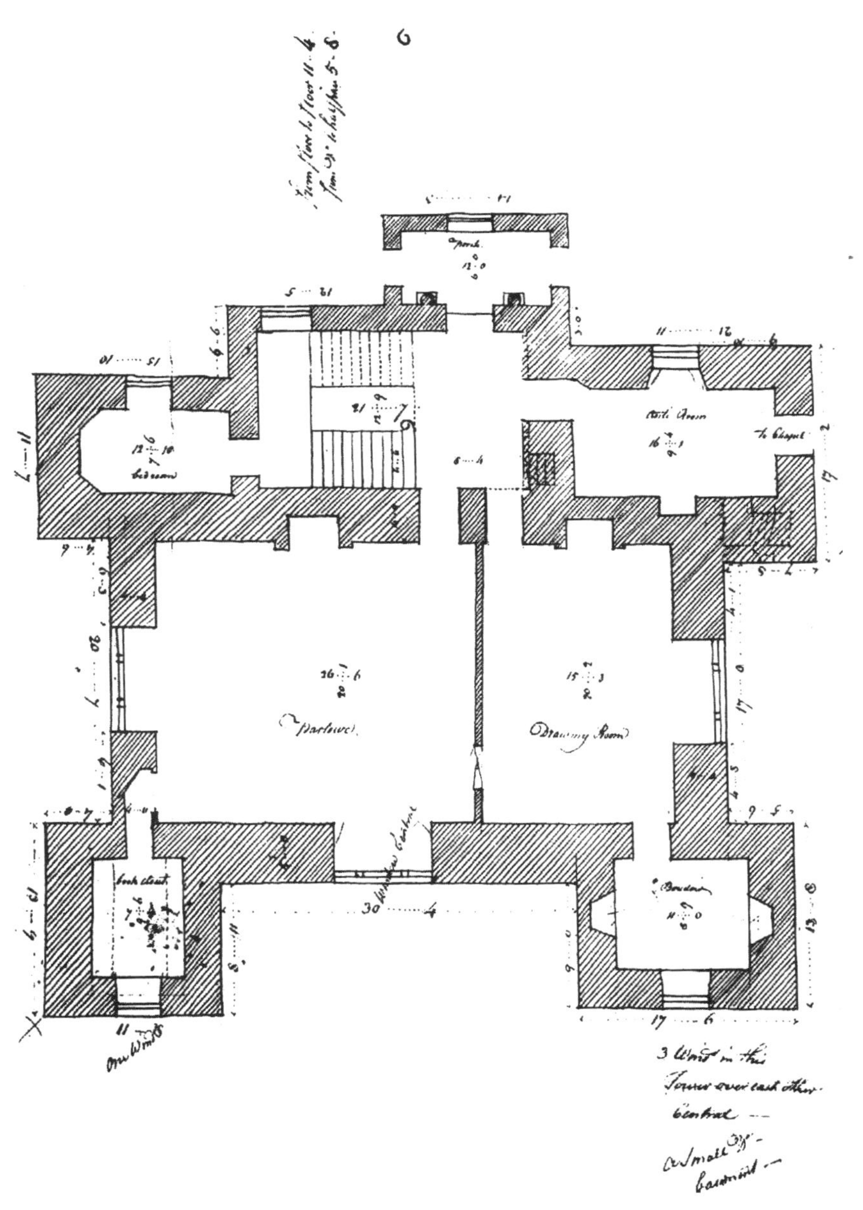

Plan of Medieval Tower House
(by kind permission of the Irish Architectural Archive)

Killeen Castle, 1813 *(Francis Johnston)*
(by kind permission of the Irish Architectural Archive)

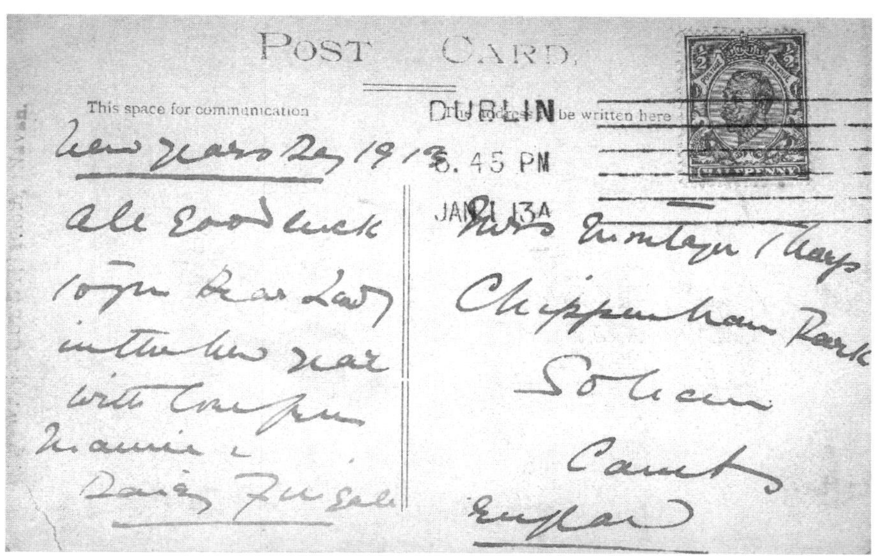

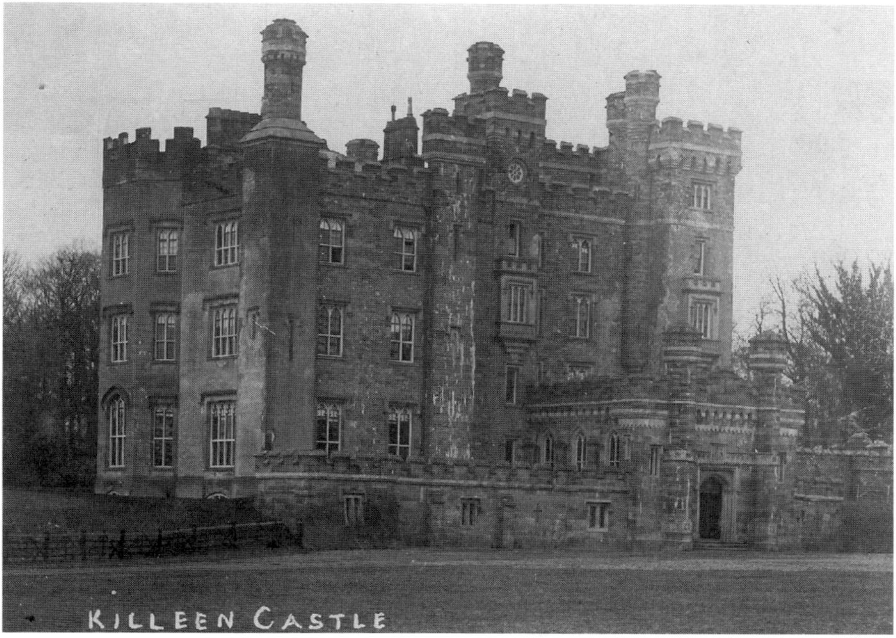

KILLEEN CASTLE

Postcard of Killeen Castle, 1913

Aerial view of Killeen.
© Clair, Countess of Fingall

Circa 1950

Aerial view of Killeen.

Circa 1950

Killeen Castle, North View
© Major and Mrs. J. Kirk

Circa 1950

Killeen Castle
(as finished by James Shiel)

1981 by Paul Tierney

Killeen Castle
(West view, Private Chapel on left)

1981 by Paul Tierney

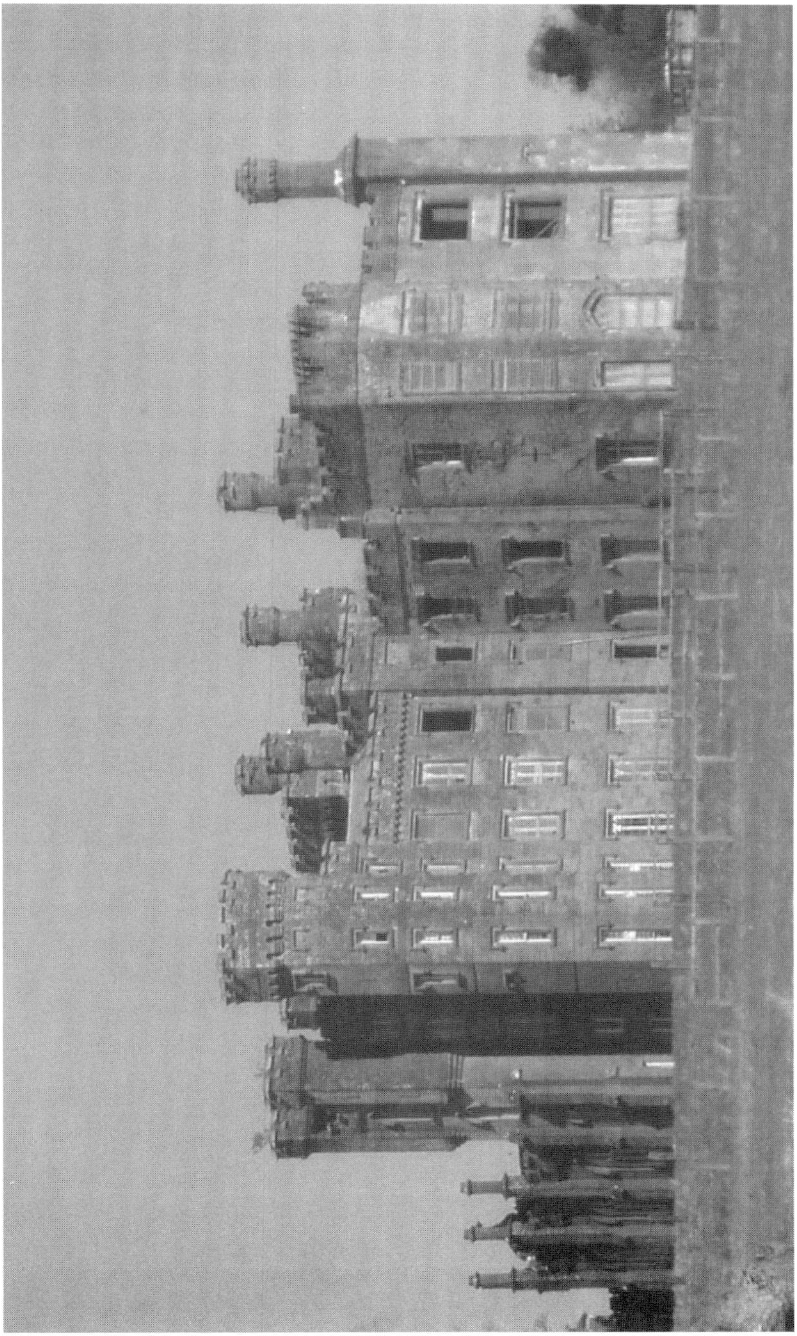

Killeen Castle
(South view, prior to restoration)

January 1995

Wollascott Family Coat of Arms

Plunkett Family Coat of Arms

Corbally Family Coat of Arms

Location: West Tower

Circa 2005

Donelan Family Coat of Arms

Restored Face

Restored Face

Location: East Façade

Circa 2005

Killeen Castle

March 2007

FIELD NAMES, WOODS & RIVER RELATING TO KILLEEN CASTLE DEMESNE

FIELD NAMES:

Ashfield
Burrow
Far Burrow
Little Burrow
Dairy Field
Decoy
Far Decoy
Lawn Pen
Upper Lawn
Lower Lime Kiln
Top Lime Kiln
Man of War
Michii Pen
Parade
Far Parade
Top Parade
River Pen
The Commons
The Orchard

WOODS:

Corp(se) Lane Wood
Dunsany Lodge Wood
Fox Den
(also known as Killeen Gorse)
Georgie's Wood
Long Wood
Russell's Wood
(also known as Stoney's Wood)

RIVER:

Rock River

LAKE:

Castle Lake

HOLY WELL:

Lady's Well

The Champion Tree at Killeen Castle

Acer Pseudoplatanus (Sycamore)

This magnificent tree, standing close to the first tee, is listed in the book of Champion Trees as one of the finest specimens in the country. It measures 6.9m in girth and 23.5m in height.

KILLEEN CHURCH

Sir Christopher Plunkett, and his wife, Joan de Cusack, erected, early in the fifteenth century, the present old church of Killeen on the site, most probably, of its predecessor. It is of Gothic Style with two towers at the West end. The east window, which is large and high, is enriched with very fine fifteenth-century tracery.

It was the Parish Church of Killeen (dedicated in honour of the Nativity of the Blessed Virgin, feast-day the 8th September). The church also would have been a place of worship for 'The Lord of the Manor', his retainers and his tenants. Mural stairs lead up to the level of a broad gallery (or rood) which was 12 or 13ft. wide. This was most likely for the use of the Lord of the Manor and his family, who could have a good view of the altar through the Chancel Arch. The latter was pointed in Killeen. The Mural staircase was entered by a neat pointed doorway in the North jamb in the Chancel Arch opening. Two-light, ogee-headed windows to North and South, gave light to the gallery and similar windows lighted the recesses below it. There is a noteworthy three-stall sedilia (seats for clergy). The sacristy-priest's residence annexe flanks the Chancel at the North-East corner. In Killeen it is two storeyed.

The church is quadrangular; separated into Chancel and Nave by a Chancel Arch of immense dimensions. The Chancel is 45½ft. internally by 19ft.10ins. The Arch is 4ft.3½ins. in depth. The Nave measures 55ft. internally by 21ft.8ins.

Some damage was done to the tombs in the church early in the 1900s. The servants of an English gentleman, who had taken Killeen Castle for a winter's hunting, placed a ladder against the outer wall of the church and from it hurled stones, with disastrous results.

Three Bishops of Meath are interred in this church.

Killeen Cemetery lies to the South side of the church.

The Church of Killeen is maintained by the Board of Works.

CHANTRY

In the West end of the Chancel a Chanty was founded consisting of four priests, to have the Holy Sacrifice of the Mass offered up for the souls of the ancestors of Sir Christopher Plunkett and Joan de Cusack. This Chantry was liberally endowed, and for several years survived the confiscations of the Reformation.

GUILD OF THE BLESSED VIRGIN

Sir Christopher Plunkett and his wife founded and endowed a confraternity of brothers and sisters under the name of the Guild of the Blessed Virgin. Application was made for legal licence and King Henry VI, by letters patent, dated the 20th July, ninth year of his reign, granted for himself and successors, to Richard Talbot, Archbishop of Dublin, that the masters, wardens, brothers and sisters of this confraternity should be regarded as a religious corporation, with a power to acquire property. Henry VII gave similar licence, and in a short time nearly one thousand acres of land were acquired. A Chantry was founded, special indulgences were obtained, a college occupying a quarter of an arce of land was erected to the West of Killeen Cemetery, and this pious confraternity became a great Catholic organisation for 'spreading knowledge, discountenancing vice, developing virtue, and diffusing the blessings of piety and charity among the people'.

LADYWELL

Tobarmurray, Tobarmuire, or Lady's Well. Stations were performed here in honour of the Blessed Virgin Mary.

Killeen Church

Circa 2000

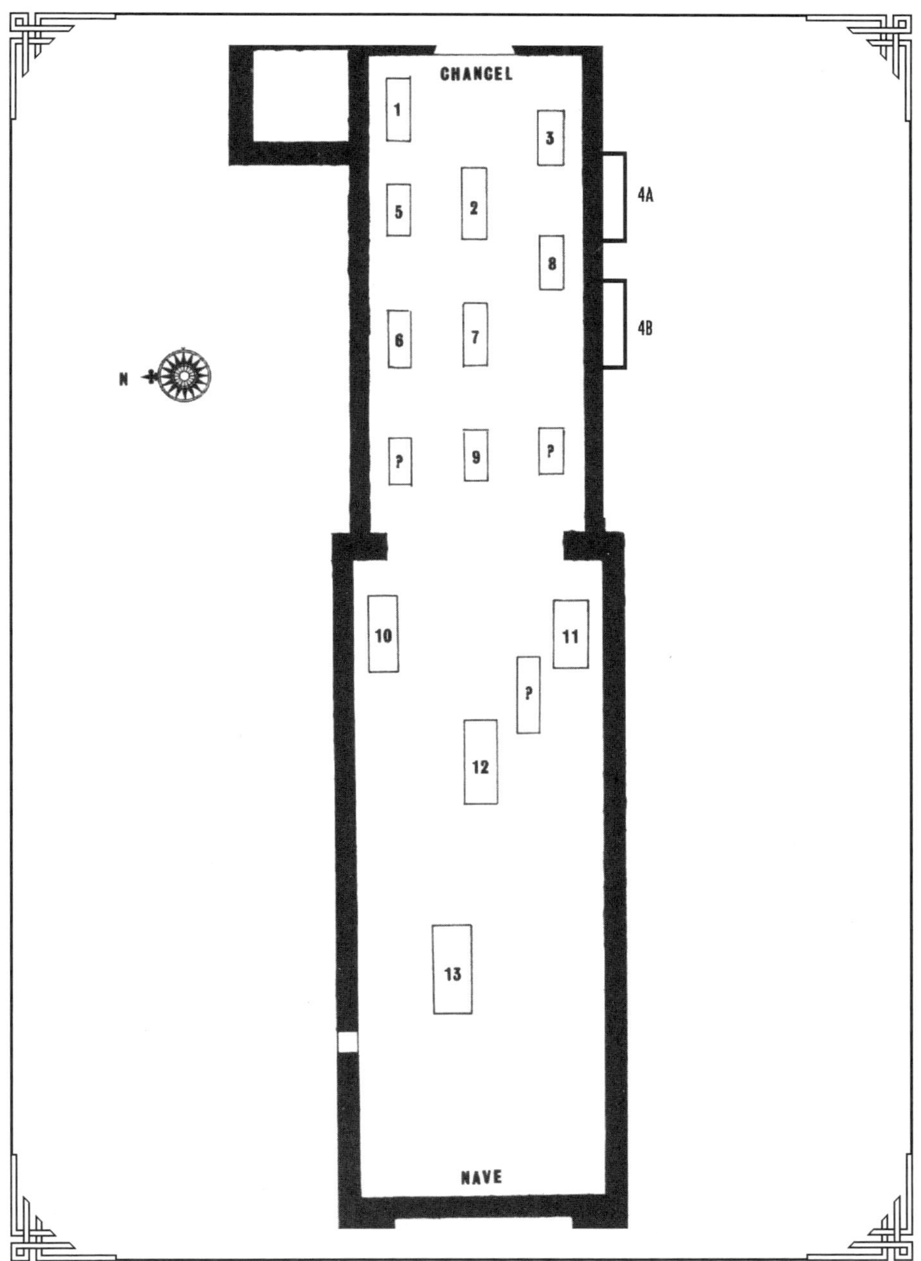

Plan of the Church and Tombs

By Paul Tierney

TOMBS OF ST. MARY'S CHURCH, KILLEEN

Extracts from notes compiled by the late Beryl F. E. Moore, M.A., M.B., in which she acknowledges Lord Walter FitzGerald's account of the Tombs in St. Mary's, Killeen, in the Memorials of the Dead (1911).

The Cross at entrance to St Mary's Church

(1) A much-fractured slab unsculptured except for a sunken portrayal of a Bishop wearing a mitre and holding a small crozier pointing outwards. The head lies to the East. A brass originally fitted into this sunken area but was lost many years ago. Such brasses are rare in Ireland.

William Silke was consecrated Bishop of Meath in 1434 and lived after that in the Palace of Ardbraccan, where he died in 1450. He is said to have been buried in Killeen Abbey in front of the altar because he had been P.P. of that Parish before being ordained Bishop of Meath. This is thought to be his grave.

Also buried here (after his long and arduous labours) are the remains of the Venerable Dr. Patrick Plunkett, second son of Christopher, 9th Lord of Killeen. Born about 1603 and died in 1679.

(2) Fingall Memorial Stone

(3) A large badly fractured slab of a Bishop wearing a mitre and holding a crozier in his left hand pointing outwards. In his right hand is a small square object, likely a book. His head lies to the East and is supported on the right side by an angel.

This grave holds many Tuites and Cusacks, who in former times were Lords of Killeen.

One of the Cusacks was Geoffrey, Bishop of Meath in the thirteenth century, who died about 1300. If this is his tombstone it is the oldest in the church.

(4) (a) This is the Plunkett-Dillon Mural Monument. The monument is in two divisions, each with a crest, coat of arms, motto and inscription.

Left-hand division ... Plunkett crest, coat of arms and motto (Festina Lente - Hasten forward with caution). Then comes inscription 'Sir Nicholas Plunkett Kt., 3rd Son of Christopher, Lord Baron of Killeen and Jane Dillon his lady, daughter to James Dillon, Lord Baron of Kilkenny West, afterwards Earle of Roscommon, died ye 27th day of December, 1680 and of his ....age the 79th.............................'.

Right-hand division ... Browne crest, coat of arms, and motto (Lux En Tour - Loyal in everything). Then comes the inscription 'This monument was erected for him by Sir Valentine Browne of Ross in ye County of Kerry, Bart. and Dame Jane his wife, sole daughter and heire of ye said Sir Nicholas Plunkett and was finished in ye month of October 1681'.

(b) In an adjacent alcove in the Chancel there is a plaque commemorating the 7th Earl and Countess, the 8th Earl and Countess and, also, the 9th Earl and Countess.

(5) This effigial slab is of the early fifteenth century. Cut in low relief and representing a knight in armour, thought to be Sir Luke Cusack, Lord of Killeen, whose heiress daughter married Sir Christopher Plunkett of Rathregan in 1401.

(6) This Plunkett-Forster Slab commemorates Edward Plunkett of Balrath, the great-grandson of the sixth son of Sir Christopher Plunkett. This Edward first married Margaret Plunkett, daughter of Christopher, Lord Dunsany, and secondly, Ellen, daughter of Richard Forster of Santry, Co. Dublin. It is dated 1584. This tomb is decorated with symbols of Our Lord's passion and crucifixion.

The lower part of the slab bears the initials E P and E F with the coats of arms of the Plunketts and Forsters. These initials stand for 'Edward Plunkett and Ellen Forster'.

(7) A knight and his lady carved in low relief surmounted by a rich double canopy. The lady is lying on her husband's right and wears a bullock's hoof-shaped headdress. Her feet rest on a cushion. The knight is clean-shaven and his feet rest on a small sporting dog. Both have their hands doubled up flat on their chests. [Feet resting on a dog signifies that the knight died peacefully in bed.]

They are Sir Christopher Plunkett and Lady Joan Cusack who married in 1401. A portion of the inscription which runs along the edge can still be read and it gives their names and says they 'Caused this church to be built'.

Some five other male Plunketts also rest in this grave.

Tomb of a Plunkett Knight and his wife. Mid-15th century. Ref. 7
© Davison & Associates Ltd.

(8) A well-preserved slab with Cusack coat of arms impaling Plunkett.

R C M P

1620

Cusack-Plunkett Arms divided by a bend

R C ... Robert Cusack M P ... Margaret Plunkett

The inscription runs round the edge of the stone and is peculiar as it starts in raised Roman capitals along one end and one side, and then continues in small letters in relief. The word 'Esquire' was left out and added above. The son's name is spelt differently to the father's, 'Cusack' being 'Cusacke'.

This Robert from Gerardstown and his wife, Margaret Porter of Kingstown, Co. Meath, had one son, James, who died two years before his father, in 1620. The tomb was likely constructed then as that date is on it. Secondly, Robert married Margaret Plunkett of Kilsaran in Co. Louth and had issue.

(9) This stone is quite plain except for an inscription round the edge in large letters in Latin. The translation is: 'Here lies the bodies of Sir Edward Plunkett Kt Lord of Dunsany, who was slain at Killaderry in Offaly in the time of the Earl of Surrey, Deputy of Ireland in AD 1521, and of Any Bermingham his wife AD 1500'.

Edward was the 4th Baron of Dunsany. He fought in the famous Battle of Knocktoe in Connaught in August, 1504. In 1521, when a much older man, he went to Killaderry in Offaly and chased after O'Carrol and O'Connor. The latter suddenly turned round and killed Sir Edward, who was brought home and buried in Killeen. O'Connor was fighting to repossess his own territory, which the Anglo-Normans had taken from his family.

There are two unidentified tombs either side of No. 9 in the Chancel.

(10) Originally this great tomb stood in the Chancel near the altar but when put together from bits and pieces scattered here and there it was placed in this alcove to save it from the weather.

It consists of two heads under a double canopy, on the left a knight in armour and, on his right, his wife in a horned headdress which was fashionable in the fifteenth century. The rest of this carved slab is gone. Around the outer edge in raised letters ran the inscription but now only the part above the lady has survived. It is: Obiter Domine Johane Cusak Domine De Killeen, Uxoris C.... The translation is: The death of Dame Joan Cusack Lady of Killeen wife of C (likely Christopher Plunkett Kt.). They were married in 1401. She died in 1441 and he in 1445. They were likely buried under No. 7.

Around the four sides are shields of many families related to the great House of Fingall by marriage in after years; St. Laurence, Le Poer, Butler and many still unidentified. There are also shields with religious emblems.

Tomb of a Plunkett Knight and his wife. Mid-15th century. Ref. 10
© Davison & Associates Ltd.

(11) An unidentified knight's effigy in higher relief than any in the Chancel, but not so elaborately carved. The hands are placed palms down on the chest, the left foot is on a small dog, no spurs are worn, and the face is clean-shaven. There is no inscription or coat of arms so it is impossible to identify him but he is likely a Plunkett of the early sixteenth century.

Effigy of Knight. Mid-15th century. Ref. 11
© Davison & Associates Ltd.

(12) An eighteenth century headstone is in the middle of the Nave, with a crucifixion at the top, while below is a scroll held by two women. It is inscribed 'Gloria in excelsis Deo'. All is in relief except the lettering. This is the tomb of the Kennedys of Crickstown, Co. Meath.

There is an unidentified tomb in the Nave between Nos. 11 and 12.

(13) In the upper portion of this slab we find good carvings of Our Lord's Passion. Below is 'INRI' - over a Latin cross. The long inscription is in raised Roman capitals except for the B's which are in small Roman capitals. The S's are reversed, the C's are like D's, the W's are written as V's and Q's are reversed P's. It runs: Here lieth the Bodi of John Quatermas and his bedfellow Ellen Rebne who rouft this porch and left an anfel for to repair the same to whose souls be merciful AD 1570.

It is not certain what 'an anfel' is, but it possibly is an 'Angel' which was a gold coin in use at that time. Also the church has no porch.

Circa 2000

THE FONT

The font was exceptionally fine and belongs to the early fifteenth century, or a little earlier. It has suffered severely from exposure and deliberate maltreatment, some of its carving having been actually hacked away.

The vessel is octagonal and stands on an octagonal column which rests in a splayed octagonal base with a central girdle-moulding. It is a large-sized font.

SIR THOMAS PLUNKETT/MARY CRUISE

KILLEEN CROSS

Sir Thomas Plunkett met his wife under very romantic circumstances. In his student days while walking in the Temple Gardens, London, he saw a beautiful girl washing clothes in the River Thames a century before the embankment was thought of. Hearing her sing in Irish a well-known ballad of the time, 'The lament of Mary Cruise', he remembered that one of his relations had murdered Sir Christopher Cruise of Rathmore, whose wife and daughter, being repudiated by their kinsfolk, had to flee from Ireland.

Young Plunkett addressed her in Irish and discovered she was the lost heiress of Rathmore. He offered her his gratuitous services as counsel when qualified, with a view to reinstating her in her proper position. The girl's mother was able to furnish the necessary documentary evidence, which ultimately enabled Plunkett to recover the estates for the family, accepting as his honorarium the hand of the heiress.

A cross still stands on the demesne of Killeen Castle as a memorial of the first visit paid to his father (Christopher, 1st Lord of Killeen) by the Lord Chief Justice and his romantically won bride; it is inscribed simply 'Thomas Plunkett - Mary Cruise'.

THE SONG OF MARY CRUISE

'Ah Blessed Mary, Hear me sighing,
On this cold stone mean labours plying;
Yet Rathmore's heiress might I name me,
And broad lands rich and many claim me,
Gilstown, Rathbeg, names known from childhood;
Fair Johnstown, hard by bog and wild wood.
Rathaffe (Blackwater near it floweth),
And Harton, where the White wheat groweth.
Kilskeer, with windows shining brightly,
Teltown, where race the coursers sprightly,
Balreask, abundant dairies showing,
Full pails and churns each day bestowing.
Thee, Ballycred, too, memory prizes,
Old Oristown to mind arises.
Caultown, near bogs, black turf providing,
Rathkenny in its "Baron" priding.

The Twelve poles, Armabregia follow,
Kilmainham of the Woody hollow.
Cruisetown with lake by sunbeams greeted,
Moydorragh gay 'mid fair woods seated.
Still could I speak of Townlands many,
Three score along the banks of the Nanny;
Twelve by the Boyne, if it were pleasure
To dwell on lost and plundered treasure'.

Sir Thomas was the third son of Sir Christopher Plunkett and Joan de Cusack. Sir Thomas was appointed Chief Justice of the King's Bench in 1461; he married twice, firstly to Genet Cusack and, secondly, Mary Cruise, daughter of Sir Christopher Cruise, of Rathmore. He died in 1471 and had issue by both wives. He is buried at Rathmore.

A descendant of Thomas Plunkett, Robert Plunkett, rode out to meet Oliver Cromwell (who had demanded that he should come to him with all his treasures) with his eleven tall sons and his one precious daughter riding behind him in the order of their ages. These were his treasures, and he produced them, hoping perhaps to soften even Cromwell's heart by such a sight. However, Robert and all his sons were killed by Cromwell's soldiers, only the girl escaped with her life.

The Cruise - Plunkett Wayside Cross
© Mrs. E. Hickey.

SAINT OLIVER PLUNKETT

The accepted date of Oliver Plunkett's birth is the 1st November, 1625, at Loughcrew, Co. Meath, about 30 miles from Killeen. The Loughcrew branch of the Plunkett Family was founded by a grandson of the 1st Lord Dunsany. Apart from being a distant cousin of the House of Fingall, Saint Oliver was also related to the Fingalls through his mother. (She was a grand-daughter of Sir Lucas Dillon, whose daughter, Genet, married Christopher, 9th Baron of Killeen.)

In his early years he was taught, probably at Killeen, by Patrick Plunkett, who later became Bishop of Meath. In 1647 Oliver went to Rome and lived there for twenty-two years as a clerical student and, later, Professor of Theology. He was ordained on the 1st January, 1654, by Bishop MacGeoghegan, at a very private ceremony in the Propaganda College, although he was a student of the Irish College.

On the 19th October, 1668, Dr. Patrick Plunkett wrote as follows to his relative Dr. Oliver Plunkett, who was then agent of the Irish Church in Rome:

'As regards your relatives, the Earls of Fingall and Roscommon have reacquired their lands and property, which were in the hands of Cromwell's Officers, and to the great delight of all friends, the Castle of Killeen ... has been restored to Lord Fingall. The Baron of Dunsany not having recovered any of his estates, is reduced to great poverty; but the Baron of Louth has obtained a partial restitution of which he lost. Mr. Nicholas Plunkett of Dunsaile, has got back all his former possessions. The other Plunketts, of Tatrath, Balrath, and Preston, have not as yet got back their castles, which are still in the hands of the Cromwellians and Londoners, having been purchased by them from the Parliament in the time of the rebellion.'

Oliver Plunkett returned to Ireland in 1670 as Archbishop of Armagh and Primate. In December, 1673, the campaign of persecution resumed, and the Bishop opted to be a fugitive in various places of refuge rather than abandon his flock.

In reference to the persecution of 1673, Dr. Oliver Plunkett remarks:

'All the convents and noviciates are destroyed, and the novices are scattered throughout the country; the last decree has also terminated the disputes of the Dominicans and Franciscans, both as to questing and as to the convents. Dr Patrick Plunkett, Bishop of Meath, on account of his old age and the gout, has, though with great difficulty received permission to remain'.

Oliver was arrested on the 6th December, 1679, and remained in close confinement in Dublin Castle. In July, 1680, there was an abortive trial in Dundalk, and he was transferred to Newgate Prison in October of the same year. In May, 1681, Oliver Plunkett was arraigned and given five weeks to bring witnesses from Ireland. On the 8th June, six days before their arrival, he was put on trial and found guilty on perjured evidence, the charge being high treason. The sentence was death, to be hanged, drawn and quartered, and this was carried out at Tyburn on the 1st July, 1681, reign of Charles II. He was the last person to be executed at Tyburn for the Catholic Faith.

Vestments belonging to Saint Oliver Plunkett were preserved in a glass-fronted cabinet in the library at Killeen Castle, and presented by the 12th Earl to Mullingar Cathedral. Another set of vestments is preserved in Manley College, Sydney, Australia, brought there by Cardinal Moran.

Blessed Oliver was canonised on the 12th October, 1975, by Pope Paul VI. The Earl and Countess of Fingall, and Lord and Lady Dunsany, attended the elevation of their Plunkett cousin.

Painting of St. Oliver Plunkett
(originally in Killeen Castle).
© Major and Mrs. J. Kirk.

DR. PATRICK PLUNKETT

Patrick Plunkett was born early in the seventeenth century, about the year 1603. His father was Christopher, ninth Lord Killeen, and his mother was Genet, or Jane, daughter of Sir Lucas Dillon. He was the second of four sons, of whom the eldest was Luke, the tenth Lord of Killeen, created Earl of Fingall, and the third the celebrated barrister Sir Nicholas Plunkett. The youngest was James.

Patrick devoted himself to the service of God from his childhood, and having entered the Cistercian order, he became, in the course of time, Abbot of St. Mary's near Dublin. Later, he served the district of Killeen and it was probably here he taught his distinguished kinsman, Oliver Plunkett.

Dr. Patrick Plunkett took an active part in all ecclesiastical movements connected with the Catholic Confederation. He became Bishop of Ardagh in the summer of 1647.

During Cromwellian times Dr. Patrick Plunkett stayed to administer to his flock but, eventually, had to seek refuge in Portugal, and from there went to France and the Netherlands. He returned to Ireland 1664/1665 and was transferred to Meath in January, 1669.

Saint Oliver Plunkett wrote the following letter to the Holy See, dated the 30th November, 1679, just days before his own arrest and imprisonment.

'To your most kind letter of the 10th of October I did not send an answer, not having any news of importance to communicate. But now I must give you the sad intelligence of the death of Dr. Patrick Plunkett, Bishop of Meath, a prelate distinguished for his birth, sincerity, integrity of life, his skill and experience in ecclesiastical matters, and his long watchfulness over his pastoral charge during the long space of thirty three years: and although he was the son of one of the first nobility of the kingdom, yet he never pursued any of the vain pleasures of this world.

He was at first Abbot of St. Mary's near Dublin. About thirty-three years ago Innocent the Tenth honoured him with the mitre of Ardagh, and Clement the Tenth transferred him to the diocese of Meath. For many years there was no other bishop in Ireland, all having fled in consequence of the fiery persecution of Cromwell. He continually enjoyed the protection or, at least, the connivance of the state, on account of his birth and moderation; he was an enemy to all temporal and political intrigues, and his nephew married to the niece of the Duke of Ormond, our Viceroy, and vice versa, one of his nieces having for her husband the nephew of the Viceroy, he had a written protection during the last two persecutions.

He died poor, because he lived rich and devoted to alm-deeds; his right hand knew not what his left hand performed; he never denied an alm to a poor man, and he gave many secret charities to the bashful poor, respectable men and widows, of whom we have a large number since the massacre of Cromwell. He had no more than 1,000 scudi (£250) when dying. All the ornaments of his chapel, and his books and pontificals, he bequeathed to me during my life, and on my death to the diocese of Meath.

He died on the 18th of this month, the day dedicated to the consecration of the Basilicas of St. Peter and St. Paul (for whom he entertained a most ardent devotion), and in the seventy-sixth year of his age; and I recommend the soul of this great prelate to your excellency when offering the Most Holy Sacrifice'.

Bishop Plunkett was buried with his ancestors in the Church of Killeen.

SIR NICHOLAS PLUNKETT

Sir Nicholas Plunkett was the third son of Sir Christopher Plunkett, 9th Baron Killeen, and brother of Dr. Patrick Plunkett, Bishop of Meath. He became an eminent barrister and a member of the Supreme Council of the Catholic Confederation.

Sir Nicholas was sent to Rome as ambassador for the Catholics of Ireland, and received a knighthood from the Holy Father, Innocent X, in 1648. During Cromwell's time he lived in exile in France and Flanders, but returned to Ireland soon after the restoration. He married Jane Dillon, daughter of James Dillon, Lord Baron of Kilkenny-West, and had an only daughter, Jane, who married Sir Valentine Brown.

In 1669 he was deputised to obtain from Charles II the restoration of the estates of the Catholic nobility of Ireland. In 1670 Sir Nicholas Plunkett was the bearer of the declaration drawn up by the National Synod of the Irish Church to His Majesty.

He died on the 27th December, 1680.

Dr. Patrick Plunkett wrote the following letter to his brother, Sir Nicholas Plunkett, on the 2nd December, 1662, from Seez (Normandy).

'Worthy Dear Brother,

> The oath taken by the nobility and yourself, I seriously considered and consulted with others. Both they and I find the same most just, lawful, and conformable to St. Paul's doctrines. For there are two sorts of obedience - the one necessary, the other voluntary. By the necessary, you ought humbly to obey the ecclesiastical superiors, and such as are authorised by them. Also, it is necessary to obey the civil superiors, as your King, and the magistrates which he has established over the country. Finally, you must obey the domestic superiors, as your father and mother, master and mistress. This obedience is called necessary, because no man can exempt himself from the duty of obeying these superiors. God having placed them in authority to command and govern, each one according to the charge which they have over

us; and to obey their command is of necessity. Voluntary obedience is that whereunto we oblige ourselves by our own election, and which is not imposed upon us by another, and of which we make no solemn vow. As a conclusion, I boldly and with an assured confidence say, our gracious King is better incomparably than such Kings as were in St. Paul's time, being infidels, yet would I have them obeyed.'

PRESCRIPTIONS & RECIPES ACCREDITED TO THE TIME OF HENRIETTA WOLLASCOTT, 7th COUNTESS OF FINGALL

PRESCRIPTIONS

INFALLIBLE CURE OF RHEUMATISM

Two ounce of Gum Guiacum [Guaiacum - resin of boxwood] in one pint of Rumm or Brandy. Let it stand 2 or 3 days to mix and dissolve - then take one spoonful in a glass of spring water every morning.

1746

AN EMULTION FOR A COUGH

Take Sperma Citi [sperm oil - oil of spermaceti whale], half an ounce, beat it in a marble mortar to a powder, then add the yolke of a new laid egg, beat them together, then add Pearl Barley Water, a pint. Put the Barley Water a little at a time so that it may be mixed well with the Sperma Citi, then strain it through a lawn sive and sweeten it with sugar. Take a wine glass when troubled with coughing.

Oct. 1757(Mrs. Rigg)

FOR A WOMAN IN LABOUR

Take oyle of nuttmeggs in dropps of white wine and ... drink.

FOR THE GOUT OR RHEUMATISM

To: W. Wollascott, Esq.

7th April, 1753

Dear Sir,

According to your desire I have sent you the Duke of Portland's receipt, this requires no other regimen, than to abstain from high sauces and French wines. W. Clarke, and my brother, joins in compliments to you and the ladies. I am,

Dear Sir, you most sincere humble servant,

M. Landsdell

Take the roots of round Birthworth, Gentian and Germanda, the tops and leaves of Ground Pine and Centaury, of each two ounces, let it be well powdered, keep it close in a bottle, take a dram of the powder every morning or evening two hours between meals in tea, water or wine.

P.S. If the powders disgree with the patient, put half an ounce of them into half a pint of Brandy. Let it stand 48 hours then pour it off, take two spoonfuls in water every morning.

RECIPES

1740-1760

TO MAKE A SALMON PYE

Take the salmon cutt it in pieces, scrape the scale off it. Season it with nutmegg, cloves, mace and salt - then putt your salmon into your pye with a pound of roast meat balls. Putt a lear of butter over the top. Chop 2 anchoves and putt them in pye. Putt in half a pint of Clarrett, half a pint of gravy then it goes into oven. When it comes out take a little gravy, little Clarrett, a little butter, 2 yolkes of eggs and putt in your pye. Shake it well and serve it up.

TO MAKE A LUMBER OYSTER PYE

Take a 100 of oysters and open and wash from the liquor. Take 12 yolkes of eggs boyled hard, a couple of chickens cutt mightly small, a handfull of two or three sweet breads cutt small, a pound of very small forced meat balls - mix all these together. Season them with nuttmegg, pepper, salt and mace. Putt them into your pye with a lear of butter on the top and butter the bottom of your dish. Pour in half a pint of gravy, cover your pye and bake it, the space of an hour exactly. When it comes out of your oven take a half pint of white wine, 2 yolkes of eggs, a little fresh butter and make it into a cordial, a little nutmegg and cutt up your pye to putt in your cordial. Shake it then serve it up.

TO MAKE SAUCE FOR A PIGG

Boyle croms of white bread in water till it thickens, then put it to some vinegar, butter and sugar to your liking, hard eggs minced, some boyled sage, grated nutmegg. Serve it to your pigg very hot or mustard to the gravy of the pigg will do as well.

TO MAKE AN ALMOND PUDDING

Talk a half a pound of Jordan almonds and blanch them, pound them in a wooden mortar very fine with a little water to keep them from burning to oyl. Boyle them in two quarts of milk for half an hour, then putt it to cool. Then beat 12 eggs with half of the whites, add a pound of white bread finely grated, sugar and spice to your liking, some sweet butter and bake it for half an hour.

TO MAKE LEMMON CREAME

Take a pint of creame, boyle half of it with a stick of cinamon. Take it off the fire and beat the yolkes of seven eggs and mix it in the creame and set it over the fire till you see it begins to thicken, then take it off and put it in the dish you intend for it, and take out the whole spice. Cut in slices candid lemon, when it is cold stick it everywhere. When it is over the fire remember to sweeten it with sugar to your liking, then the other half pint put half the juice of a lemon and sugar to your liking, whip it up and lay it on with a spoon.

GLOSSARY

ARRAIGNED	...	called to account - put on trail
ATTAINTED	...	lost civil rights through conviction for high treason (corruption of blood)
ATTEST	...	to testify or bear witness to - to affirm by signature or oath
CUSTOS ROTULORUM	...	Guardian of the Rolls
DISENTAILED	...	To break the entail (rule of descent) of an estate
FIEF	...	land held in fee, or on condition of military service
JOINTURE	...	property settled on a woman at marriage to be enjoyed after her husband's death
PALE	...	area within (approximately) 30 miles of Dublin where royal authority was enforced
SOCAGE	...	tenure of lands by service fixed and determinate in quality

SOURCES

Putting the Cill into Killeen
Christine Baker
Archaeology Ireland
Winter 2006

Battlements & a Castle Air
Bernadette Goslin
R.I.A.I. Bulletin
September, 1984

Blessed Oliver Plunkett
Historical Studies
Fr. Paul Walsh
Published by Gill (Dublin)
1937

Burke's Peerage

Champion Trees
Published by the Tree Council of Ireland - 2005

Clair, Countess of Fingall

Randal, 19th Lord Dunsany

Fingal County Archives Service

Fitz.Gerald & Associates Architects

Genealogical Office

Mrs. Elizabeth Hickey

Irish Medieval Figure Sculpture 1200-1600
John Hunt with assistance and contributions from Peter Harbison
Published by the Irish University Press - 1974

Irish Tatler & Sketch
October, 1950

Major & Mrs. J. Kirk

Ms. Ruth Lawler

Dr. Beryl F. E. Moore
A Guide to Killeen with Memorial Inscriptions. Undated Typescript.

National Library of Ireland

Ordnance Survey Office

Primary Valuation
1848-1865

John & Sue Richardson

Ríocht na Mídhe
Various Articles

St. Mary's Church Woolhampton
Dom Geoffrey Scott, O.S.B.
Published 1975

Seventy Years Young Memories of Elizabeth, Countess of Fingall
First published by Collins of London in 1937
Paperback edition first published in 1991 by The Lilliput Press Ltd. in association with Carty/Lynch

Snowbury Ltd.

The Cusack Family of Co. Meath & Dublin
Hubert Gallwey
Articles in Irish Genealogist

The Diocese of Meath
Rev. A. Cogan
Volume I published 1862
Volume II published 1867
Volume III published 1870

The Kin of Blessed Oliver
Fr. Paul Walsh
Catholic Bulletin
December, 1935

The Letters of Saint Oliver Plunkett edited by Monsignor John Hanly
Published by Dolmen Press
1979

The Weekly Irish Times
September 12th, 1936

Mr. Paul Tierney

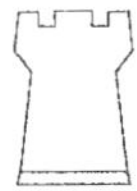

ACKNOWLEDGEMENTS

Ms. Christine Baker
Fr. J. Bird
Mr. & Mrs. B. Brindley
Mr. & Mrs. G. Briscoe
Mr. & Mrs. Paddy Carroll
Fr. A. Doyle
Mr. Sean Dungan
Lord & Lady Dunsany
Mr. Antony Farrell
Earl & Countess of Fingall
Mr. Sean Flynn
Mr. Hubert Gallwey
Fr. J. Garvey
Ms. Bernadette Goslin
Mrs. Anne Gray
Monsignor John Hanly
Mr. Peter Harbison
Mrs. Elizabeth Hickey
Ms. Fiona Hoey
Mrs. Maureen Hoey
Mr. Noel Kerrigan
Major & Mrs. J. Kirk
Mr. Philip MacDermott
Mr. Colm McQuinn
Dr. Beryl F. E. Moore
Mr. Frank Moore
Lt. Col. W. L. Newell
Mr. Micheal O'Brien
Ms. Eiske Rahill
Staff of Fingal County Archives Service & Libraries
Staff of Genealogical Office
Staff of Meath County Library
Staff of The Irish Architectural Archive
Staff of National Library of Ireland
Mr. & Mrs. C. von Schmieder
Mr & Mrs. Christopher Slattery
Snowbury Ltd.
Mr. David Sweetman
Mr. Paul Tierney